## Praise for *Letting My Light Shine*

It's a daunting task to analyze one's own life through the filter of God's viewpoint. Luverne's Nancy Petrey shares her life with candor and joy. It has been shaped by music and by her deep faith.

Nancy tells of her time growing up in a sweet and safe American small town, of the popular music she and her friends loved and the church music that inspired them. We learn of her beloved husband Curtis, and their life together.

My favorite parts of the book are those when she relates her experiences and life with biblical lessons. These are her particular strengths as a writer. Her final chapter ties all these threads of love and music and faith into a satisfying conclusion.

Every life, no matter how ordinary, is made extraordinary when God is allowed to work through us. That is Nancy Petrey's most important lesson for us.

**Rev. Dave (Doc) Kirby**
Pastor, Pine Level United Methodist Church
Full-time lecturer,
Hall School of Journalism & Communication, Troy University
Operations & Program Manager,
Troy Broadcasting Corporation,
Troy, Alabama.
Chaplain, Camp Kirkland's Metro Big Band of Nashville, TN

I loved your book. Your life has been a light in the darkness. As I turned the pages, I laughed and sometimes cried, yet the presence of the Holy Spirit flowed from the page in the sweetest notes.

*"Heard melodies are sweet, but those unheard are sweeter"—Keats.*
**Theresa M. Johnson, Ph.D.**
Senior Lecturer of English and Director of Teaching English
to Speakers of Other Languages (TESOL)
Troy University, Troy, Alabama

I sat down to read this afternoon and couldn't stop! ... I am reading a great story and very much feel drawn into your life.... I feel it is a life well lived for Jesus (as you point out we are His workmanship, His poem), and it shows how His hand guides all the way.... I absolutely loved it and did not want it to end. ... I have to say that I am also amazed at your life and all the ways that our precious Lord has led you and used you and prepared you to bring Him glory. ... I had to have Kleenex in hand for Chapter 40. It was bittersweet indeed. I was thinking how the Lord had Curtis move home and how the purchase of the grand piano and Curtis' promotion of your music were all preparing you for life without Curtis - a life that still honors and brings glory to God. ...

**Barbara Renacker**, Retired School Teacher
Columbus, Mississippi

# Letting My Light Shine

### Musical Memoirs

### Nancy Petrey

Energion Publications
Gonzalez, Florida
2018

ISBN10: 1-63199-531-6
ISBN13: 978-1-63199-531-6
Library of Congress Control Number: 2018942673

Energion Publications
P. O. Box 841
Gonzalez, FL 32560
850-525-3916


energionpubs.com
pubs@energion.com

# DEDICATION

This book is dedicated to my mother, Nan Marley Williams,
and to my husband, Curtis Petrey.

In my musical pursuits, whether playing the piano or singing,
Mother was my greatest encourager,
and later Curtis assumed that role.
They both promoted me and were proud of me.
Mother passed on to me her musical talent
and had the greatest influence on my piano playing.
She and Daddy footed the bill for sixteen years of piano lessons.
Curtis was an awesome man, a gift of God to me, all his family,
and the churches he served as pastor.

As I have said many times,
he was "THE WIND BENEATH MY WINGS."
I know he and Mother are standing in the balcony of heaven
And continuing to cheer me on.

I pray this book will cheer on all musical performers,
especially those who acknowledge the Lord
as the Giver of music.
Thank you, Mother,
my loving and faithful nurturer and example.

Thank you, Curtis, my lover and my best friend.

# TABLE OF CONTENTS

# ACKNOWLEDGMENTS

It has been a joy writing this book. My research in my journals, photo albums, and in emails to friends and relatives has turned up rich memories. I pray my children, grandchildren, and posterity will find their musical heritage through me a treasure and will pass it on.

It seems to me that piano playing is becoming a lost art because of increasing concentration on the electronic keyboard and guitars, especially in church music. School children are pursuing other activities, including dancing lessons, band, and sports of all kinds. They often begin piano lessons but drop out after a few years, either losing interest or not being able to balance their piano lessons and other activities. Many people have said to me, "I wish I had kept on with my piano lessons." But by then they are adults with too many responsibilities to devote to learning the piano. Piano study is a time-consuming and solitary "sport." To attain any proficiency there is a price to be paid. I praise the piano teachers who are still plying their trade and turning out the good pianists we do have.

Oh, how I miss my husband Curtis who proofread in segments everything I have written! He was a great encourager, even though most of the time his only comment after reading a chapter would be "It's good." Now I must rely on friends and my children to proofread for me.

I wish to acknowledge these people for their help in proofreading and suggestions: Jacquelyn Hodges Earnest, David Williams, Hannah May, Susan Petrey Carriker, Jim Petrey, Bert Petrey, Theresa Johnson, and Barbara Renacker. I asked Barbara to be my prayer warrior as I was writing the book and to proofread it at the conclusion. Her accolades have sent my spirit soaring! That was a great sacrifice of her time, and I appreciate it so much. Others have prayed for me as I wrote the book, and their prayers surely got good results. I thank them.

Special thanks goes to Buddy Johnson, our Minister of Music at South Luverne Baptist Church. He put me in contact with Rev. Dave (Doc) Kirby, his friend who has impressive credentials at Troy University and has read thousands of books and interviewed authors on the radio. I am very thankful for his glowing endorsement of my book, but especially thankful for Buddy and for his wife Theresa, an English Professor at Troy University, who also wrote a fine endorsement for my book.

I especially thank my son-in-law, Conrad Carriker, for making a video of me, playing "Fantaisie Impromptu," which got thousands of views on Facebook! Conrad helped in other technical ways also. I want to thank Lisa Perritt for making a video of me, October 2015, at The Cove, playing "Revolutionary Etude" by Chopin. Thank you also to Jan White for making the video of me, playing "Battle Hymn of the Republic" at First Baptist Church in Andalusia, Alabama, on June 21, 2016. For your listening pleasure, you can find the links to these performances in the footnotes in Chapter 40. Steve Rapp put online one of my praise tapes from the 1980s, and the link is in Chapter 19. I appreciate Steve for preserving what I consider a treasure. (There's a great story about Steve in Chapter 21.)

Finally, I am always grateful for my publishers, Henry and Jody Neufeld, who believe in me and are enthusiastically publishing this, my fifth book. The number 5 is the number of grace. God's grace is truly amazing!

# PREFACE

My purpose in writing this book is to shine a spotlight on the One who gave me my musical talent, several outstanding teachers to help me develop it, and people, primarily a husband, to promote it. It is a story that shows how the Lord opens doors and uses music to bring blessings to others and to bring pleasure and glory to Himself. My life verse has been *"Let your light so shine before men, that they may see your good works and* **give glory to your Father in heaven***"* (Matthew 5:16).

*"The Lord takes pleasure in His people"* (Psalm 149:4). He really does. Jesus told us we are to shine forth His light, and that we should not hide our light under a basket but to put it on a lampstand to give light to all in the house (Matthew 5:14-15). With that in mind I have written my musical memoirs covering 73 years!

Who wants to read the memoirs of an ordinary person like me? Since I am not a celebrity or a notorious person, why would anyone care about my life story? My answer also applies to you. You are unique. No one else's life is like yours. As a member of God's royal family through my adoption by His Son, Jesus Christ (I hope that applies to you), I am God's "workmanship" (Ephesians 2:10). The Greek word for that means "poem." If my life is a poem, it needs to be read!

In the area of music, I will unashamedly say that I have shared the gift God gave me and have let my light shine for the purpose of glorifying Him, my Maker and Redeemer. This book is meant to be a heritage for my family and a means of saying "thank you" to all the wonderful people God has used in my life to help me shine His light more brightly.

Just because a person is gifted by God does not indicate superiority or ranking in His sight. I am a frail human being with many faults. Nevertheless, I can say with Paul, *"But we have this treasure in earthen vessels, that the excellence of the power may be of God and not of us"* (2 Corinthians 4:7).

I mention a whole lot of names in this book. Please forgive me if I failed to mention your name, even though I may have mentioned the names of people in the same time period and place as you were.

It is my prayer that you will enjoy reading this book and will pass on to others the light and love of God through the gifts He has given you. *"It only takes a spark to get a fire going, and soon all those around will warm up in its glowing. That's how it is with God's love, once you've experienced it. You spread His love to everyone — you want to PASS IT ON."[1]*

---

1    1969 Bud John Songs, Inc., Words and Music by Kurt Kaiser

# Chapter 1

## Sioux City Sue

My earliest memory of a musical performance was the night my mother pushed me out in front of the curtain on the stage of Luverne High School, in Luverne, Alabama, where she was a teacher, and told me to sing! I was five years old, and I was terrified! All the crowd noise quieted down when it became obvious the little girl was about to do something. Although the spotlight blinded me, I knew a big auditorium full of people was staring at me! I managed to squeak out a quick rendition of "Sioux City Sue" and return to a safe place behind the curtain. Fear kept me from enjoying whatever applause resulted. I assume there was some applause for my heroic efforts, but I can't remember!

*Sioux City Sue, Sioux City Sue,*
*Your hair is red, your eyes are blue,*
*I'd swap my horse and dog for you,*
*Sioux City Sue, Sioux City Sue,*
*There ain't no gal as true*
*As my sweet Sioux City Sue![2]*

The real show the audience had come to see must have been delayed, and I was a convenient "filler." I probably will never know the reason for my musical debut. Nevertheless, my musical career was launched in a quite unlikely way, thanks to my proud mother, Nan Elizabeth Marley Williams. "Miss Nan" was the pianist for every skit and program in the high school in Luverne, Alabama. She would continue to put me on stage through my school years at every opportunity.

---

Dick Thomas & Ray Freedman, © July 1945 New York City

I began piano lessons with Mrs. Ethel Tankersley at Luverne Grammar School in the first grade at age five. Miss Ethel's hair was red, but she was not Sioux City Sue. In my eyes she appeared ancient, not a cute girl that someone would swap his horse and dog for! However, she would be my piano teacher for twelve years, and she laid a good foundation for my musical education.

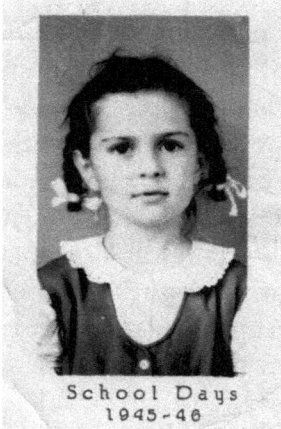

School Days
1945-46

Nancy Williams in first grade at Luverne Elementary School, Luverne, Alabama - 1945-46

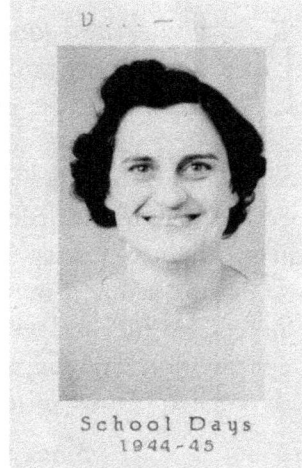

School Days
1944-45

Nan Marley Williams, teacher at Luverne High School, my mother

Mrs. Ethel Tankersley, my first piano teacher

# CHAPTER 2

## SMALL BEGINNINGS

My maternal grandmother "Ma-Ma," Ada Marley, had made sure that her daughter, Nan Elizabeth, had piano lessons, and that same determination was in my mother who chose Miss Ethel as the one to give her children piano lessons. Mother grew up playing on a baby grand piano, so she had a baby grand piano in our home for herself, my older brother David, and me.

Miss Ethel Jones (1874-1961) graduated from Judson College and began teaching piano and voice in Luverne. She married Dr. Felix Marcus Tully Tankersley, Jr. (1862-1922), a physician who later became Probate Judge in Crenshaw County. When I became her student, Miss Ethel, a widow, had been teaching piano and voice in Luverne for

My mother Nan and grandparents, David Caswell and Ada Marsh Marley, ca. 1924

Bertie & Nan Williams with children - Nancy, Ben, and David - 1948

many years and was already a legend. She also directed the choir at First Baptist Church in Luverne and held that position approximately 50 years. She was a professional and dressed like one, but her red hair was her most distinguishing feature. It was wavy and styled close to her head with little corkscrew sideburns, called "spit curls!" She was a large and formidable figure sitting erect in her chair at the right side of the piano, wielding her cedar pointer with precision. To make a "passionate point," she would slap the pointer on the page, saying something like, "I told you to watch your fingering!" Or she would warn, "You must practice your scales!" I was one of the lucky ones who rarely, if ever, had a rap on the knuckles for some musical transgression. My brother and many others did not escape the wrath of the pointer, however, and on occasion would even receive a heavy-handed pat on the back. Some parents were too weak-kneed to turn their children over to Miss Ethel and chose instead to enroll them with Mrs. Roberta Little. Miss Roberta had been Miss Ethel's pupil. She was also the organist at the First Baptist Church, so all was well. Miss Ethel had out-of-town students, however, signifying her "fame."

I can remember Miss Ethel's studio in the grammar school across the street from my daddy's cotton warehouse, Planters Trading Company, in downtown Luverne. One entrance to the studio was via tall stairs outside the building. The only vivid memory I have of that particular studio was when Miss Ethel used a bouncing ball to teach rhythm. This building burned down when I was in the fifth grade, and the new studio was relocated to Luverne High School. This studio was accessed both by tall stairs outside the building and from a hall on the north side of the school. Her studio was moved eventually to the concrete block building near the football field, where it had formerly been used by the football team. The building became a duplex, with Miss Roberta's studio side by side with Miss Ethel's.

My first piano book was *Teaching Little Fingers to Play* by John Thompson, and my first piece was "Here We Go Up a Row to a Birthday Party," three notes played with the right hand and then with the left hand. When I could finally play the last piece in the book, "From a Wigwam," and proceed to *Book One*, I felt like I had arrived! Years later, I attended a Sandi Patti concert and found out that I was indeed in good company. Sandi Patti sat at the piano and demonstrated her early piano lessons, playing songs from the John Thompson books I had used! As the Bible says, *"Do not despise these small beginnings ... "* (Zechariah 4:10, NLT).

# CHAPTER 3

## THE RECITAL

Miss Ethel groomed us all year long for a recital at the end of the school year. We knew early on which pieces would be "the recital pieces." The recital was held in the Luverne High School auditorium, and we played on a big grand piano which graced the huge stage and was flanked by a flower arrangement. This was a much-dreaded affair. Stage fright was a tangible thing like the "big bad wolf." The girls dressed up in their best dresses. Mine was a white organdy dress. This was a serious performance, even if one's piece was only the birthday party song. Miss Ethel had recitals for the different age groups. The little people went first. She had rows of chairs for us backstage. The darkness backstage fit our mood. The auditorium was filled with admiring parents and other relatives and friends, ready to do their duty in smiling and clapping after each child's performance.

As each recital progressed Miss Ethel would indicate when your time had come to perform. As I recall, she placed the children who excelled and had more advanced pieces at the last. In the higher grades, I seemed to be placed closer to the end, which I hated. The torture of waiting was almost unbearable. Then the time would come for each of us to walk out on the big stage to "the gallows." Amazingly, with rare exceptions, each child did well, including me, and each smiled, bowed and returned backstage a hundred pounds lighter!

Memorization was the toughest aspect of playing the piano. While waiting for our turn, we little performers were always muttering, "I hope I don't forget. I hope I don't forget." Once in a while, this horror would transpire, and there was much comforting to be done by those who had not yet gone to "the chopping block," or by those who had gone but returned intact.

My brother David persevered through ten years of piano lessons until the fateful night when his musical career abruptly ended. Here is his story to me in his own words:

> *How could I forget my embarrassment at our recital when I was in the 10th grade? The selection was a modern composition named "Holiday," and I'd never played it completely through, even when practicing at home. Looking back, it seems unbelievable that I thought I could play it to completion under the pressure of a recital. Anyhow, I was playing along and hit a discord. To correct an error, it was always necessary for me to start from the beginning. But this time I was so far along in the piece, that I attempted to correct the discord then and there. Well, I hit another discord. Realizing that the odds that I would succeed with another try were infinitesimal, I looked at the audience, smiled a little, arose from the bench, and walked back to where you all were sitting offstage. Miss Ethel's eyes were wet with tears as she looked at me and said, "You did well, son." That was my last performance. Only God knows how Miss Ethel was affected.*

Like my brother, I did not escape the embarrassment of memory loss during a piano performance, but it would happen after my high school years (see Chapter 11).

# CHAPTER 4

## MISS ETHEL'S DOS AND DON'TS

Classical pieces were Miss Ethel's delight. She introduced her students to the great composers, such as Johannes Bach, Joseph Haydn, Ludwig van Beethoven, Johannes Brahms, Franz Liszt, and Amadeus Mozart. We learned "Air" by Joseph Haydn in our first book, *Teaching Little Fingers to Play.* "Papa Haydn" was immortalized in our little hearts with the words and catchy tune:

*Papa Haydn's dead and gone*
*but his memory lingers on.*
*When his mood was one of bliss*
*he wrote jolly tunes like this.*

My brother David learned to play Mozart's "Sonata No. 1 in C," and he could really rip it off at high speed! But no one could match my speed in "Minute Waltz" by Chopin! After a recital, a relative made a comment something like this, "Well, you did play it in a minute! You ran away with it." As a little girl, I basked in these words, considering them a high compliment. The truth was that the faster I played a piece, the less likely I would have a memory lapse! I wanted it over as quickly as possible!

Yes, classical music was at the top of Miss Ethel's list of "dos" in our education. Scales were next on that list, both major and minor scales, which she insisted we keep a record of in a spiral notebook. I never did understand the importance of playing scales until college. After all, scales were the building blocks of every single composition. At that time, I quickly learned them all, lest I be discovered as an illiterate pianist who dared to major in piano! For each scale

Miss Ethel taught us arpeggios (the notes of chords played one at the time up and down the keyboard for several octaves) and inversions (rearrangement of the notes) of chords.

Miss Ethel had a list of "don'ts" also. She forbade her students to play "by ear," because she feared it would lead to musical illiteracy, the inability to read music from the musical score. I wasn't tempted in that way because I did not have a natural "bent" for playing by ear, and I enjoyed reading music anyway. I became a good sight reader. Just like reading books can take you places you would never go yourself, the adventure of reading new music feels the same.

My mother had drawers full of popular music. I considered it a treasure trove, and I began to try it out in my teenage years. I never mentioned any of this to Miss Ethel, assuming she would not approve. Some of my favorites were "Blue Moon," "That Old Black Magic," and "Tea for Two." On the ukulele I learned to play "Five Foot Two," "Eyes of Blue" and "Ain't She Sweet." Had Miss Ethel known about my "shadowy" activities, she would have cringed! To her, these songs would be like comic books compared to the great literary classics. I'm sure she knew about it, however, but she never mentioned it.

Another item on the "dos" list was finger exercises from books by Hanon and Czerny. This was sheer boredom. However, to play the classical pieces Miss Ethel assigned, our fingers had to be flexible and strong. These exercises were necessary for musical fitness in the same way that a treadmill and weights are for physical fitness.

The final and most important thing on Miss Ethel's list of "dos" was PRACTICE! That was by far the hardest thing of all. To fulfill this requirement, you would have to be a hermit! Needless to say, I failed miserably. When lesson time came, which was twice a week for thirty minutes each, I would try my best to fake it. Sometimes I succeeded, and sometimes I didn't. I hated to answer the dreaded question, "Have you practiced?" Since my conscience wouldn't let me lie, and I couldn't answer in the affirmative, I prayed hard she wouldn't ask me. Sometimes I would plead, "Well, I practiced

**some**, but not **every** day." Somehow, I escaped Miss Ethel's wrath. Poor David was not so fortunate.

This was the routine: when my lesson time came around, I would go and stand at her studio door and wait for the student before me to leave. My inevitable question to him or her was, "Is she in a good mood?" If the answer was no, and I had barely touched the piano all week, I would tremble with anxiety and sheepishly enter the studio, not sure what my fate would be.

Actually, Miss Ethel was mostly "all bark and no bite." She did have a good sense of humor, and it probably saved her life from endless monotony, being subjected to wrong notes day in and day out. I still smile when I remember her statement of light scolding, "Now ain't you a bird!" I am indebted to her for setting high standards and assigning me beautiful pieces of music way beyond my ability to learn. Her confidence in me helped me to achieve the seemingly impossible in musical performance even to this day.

Whatever pieces Miss Ethel assigned me I had to learn, but the ones I really liked got the most practice. My favorites were those by Frederic Chopin, especially "Fantaisie Impromptu," "Revolutionary Etude," and "Minute Waltz." I was in senior high school when I learned "Fantaisie Impromptu." After a dormant period of decades, I re-memorized it. It became part of my repertoire when I obtained a gorgeous grand piano of my own in 2002. My husband Curtis liked it, too. He called it "Rainbows," because "I'm Always Chasing Rainbows," a popular song adapted from the middle section of the Chopin piece, was familiar to him.[3] (See Chapters 32 and 37 for a testimony about the grand piano and performances of this piece.)

It is astounding that hundreds, maybe thousands, of popular songs are based on classical compositions.[4] I have discovered that classical music has influenced popular music far beyond what any-

---

3   "I'm Always Chasing Rainbows," words by Joseph McCarthy, music by Harry Carroll, 1917, later recorded by many singers, including Judy Garland in 1941.

4   http://www.magle.dk/music-forums/940-modern-popular-songs-based.html

one could imagine! For a **long** list of popular songs drawn from themes of classical pieces, dating from 1891 to 2005, look at http://www.solopassion.com/node/971.

It could be considered a compliment to the great master composers that millions of people have heard their musical themes because songwriters in modern times have borrowed them. It attests to the timelessness of truly great music. On the other hand, it is sad that rarely are the original composers given any credit for the inspiration they have provided. What a blessing classical music is, and what a blessing teachers are who assign the masters' compositions to their students. I am grateful to Miss Ethel.

# CHAPTER 5

## TRAIN UP A CHILD

Have you ever considered that your abilities, whether musical or nonmusical, were determined before you were born? You weren't born into a certain family by accident, nor was your place of birth just happenstance. Scripture sheds light on why you are who you are, why you have a certain family and live in a certain place. The Apostle Paul told the Athenians that God had created all nations and determined their boundaries (Acts 17:26). Not only your nationality was ordained, but God determined your purpose in life. Your abilities and accomplishments have a purpose. *"Let your light so shine before men that they may see your good works and **give glory to your Father in Heaven**"* (Matthew 5:16). I ended my high school valedictory address with that verse, and I continually pray it may be so for me and my family.

Therefore, if God **created** each person with a specific purpose in mind so that He might be glorified, then we should seek out what He wants to do **in** us and **through** us in life.

*You made all the delicate, inner parts of my body*
*and knit me together in my mother's womb.*
*Thank you for making me so wonderfully complex!*
*Your workmanship is marvelous—how well I know it.*
*You watched me as I was being formed in utter seclusion,*
*as I was woven together in the dark of the womb.*
*You saw me before I was born.*
*Every day of my life was recorded in your book.*
*Every moment was laid out*

*before a single day had passed.*
(Psalm 139:13-16, NLT)

Every day recorded? Wow! My husband Curtis used to say that when we messed up God's perfect plan for our lives, He had alternate plans. How comforting. Another verse makes it clear that God planned for us to do certain things: *"For we are His workmanship, created in Christ Jesus for good works, which God prepared beforehand that we should walk in them"* (Ephesians 2:10).

If we have developed our God-given abilities and accomplished anything, we need to give God the credit. Also, we should look back and see which people God chose to help us achieve His purposes. He will give us eyes to see His hand in our lives if we ask.

As for Miss Ethel, I do praise God for her. Someone told me that they observed her each week day, standing in front of her house in the dark before the sun rose to get a taxi to take her to school. That image speaks volumes. Her dedication in teaching music to children should be recognized by all her students, but how many ever thought of her sacrifices for us?

Today when I sit at my grand piano in Petrey and play whatever my heart desires, I remember Miss Ethel, my mother, and two other piano teachers who helped make me what I am today as a pianist, seeking to glorify God for this gift. In relation to music, my parents and my piano (and voice) teachers helped fulfill this truth: *"Train up a child in the way he should go: and when he is old, he will not depart from it"* (Proverbs 22:6, KJV).

# CHAPTER 6

## MUSICAL EXPLOITS IN HIGH SCHOOL DAYS

Besides the music Miss Ethel assigned me, I learned many popular songs on my own, and I began to buy sheet music to add to Mother's stack. No one had to beg or threaten me to learn the latest hits. I was lost in romantic fantasies as I played and sang my heart away. Some of those songs that mesmerized me the most as I dreamed of teenage romance were "P.S. I Love You," "Secret Love," "My Own True Love," "Outside of Heaven," and "Wanted." There were many others, but to list them would take half a book!

Elvis Presley came on the scene in the 1950s, and rock music was born, but this was not the type of music I preferred. I did sing some of these songs, however, such as "Rock Around the Clock," "Blue Suede Shoes," and a milder one, "Love Me Tender." By today's standards, Elvis Presley's early performances are not considered R-rated, but I was a very sheltered young girl, and, frankly, I was shocked at his gyrations! My boyfriend, Curtis Petrey, listened to "Randy's Record Shop" on the radio late at night, but that music did not appeal to me either. The singers I preferred were Perry Como, Vic Damone, Eddie Fisher, Debbie Reynolds, Doris Day, Andy Williams, and Tony Bennett, to name a few. I did learn some of the novelty songs, such as "Transfusion" and "Speedo," which had funny lyrics. My brother David and his friends, Warren Lightfoot, Lewis Gholston, and Leo Phillips, did a hilarious job of pantomiming "Transfusion" for a program at Luverne High. David was in another quartet which made a hit at Beta Club Convention in Birmingham. Their repertoire included "Hello, My Baby," "I

Get So Lonely," "Tina Marie," and others. Those were wonderful days in high school.

Music filled our home. Both Mother's family and Daddy's family were talented in music. Besides my own mother, Aunt Lila, Daddy's sister, could really tear up a piano. At family gatherings at our house, Aunt Lila and Mother would take turns playing the piano, and I would stand as close as possible to soak up the good "oldies" music. Aunt Era, my daddy's sister-in-law, and his sister Ruth would gather around to sing, too. "Am I Blue?" is one song I remember that Aunt Lila played. Mother played, "The World is Waiting for the Sunrise." Of course, we sang the old hymns, too. That was more my daddy's style.

When our family went to Brundidge to visit Mother's brother, Escar Marley, wife Helen, and their children, Elizabeth Ann and David, there was more piano playing. Elizabeth Ann was a virtuoso on piano, violin, organ, and she was also a singer and composer! (Today at 85, she is still playing the church organ, violin, piano, and teaching students.) She taught me how to play the "Boogie Woogie." Her version had a mean left hand, and I had quite a ball with it.

David Marley played the cornet and trumpet. I once accompanied him on "Cherry Pink and Apple Blossom White." That was at a Talent Show at Huntingdon College when we attended Assembly in the summer of 1956. My number was Chopin's "Revolutionary Etude." It was very difficult to play because one of the participants, who was dressed up as a clown, decided he would kneel down by the piano and use a fan to cool off my fingers as they ripped up and down the keyboard at lightning speed! He was trying to steal the show, and it made David mad. As it turned out David won first prize in the talent contest, and I won second prize!

I was exposed to lots of popular music at home, but Mother also exposed us to some of the most beautiful **classical** music ever written. She played phonograph recordings of Sergei Rachmaninoff's *Piano Cocerto No. 2* and Tchaikovsky's *Piano Concerto No.*

*1 in B Flat Minor* over and over. This music inspired my soul to greater depths than I had ever known.

Mrs. Evelyn Turner, my English teacher and family friend, teamed up with Mother in high school to create musical skits and plays. I marveled at my mother's ability to sight read the piano music for the musicals Miss Evelyn chose for her famed annual Senior Play. There were also Beta Club skits that almost always brought home first prize at the annual Beta Club Convention in Birmingham. Staying in the Tutwiler Hotel was the worldliest adventure I had experienced at that time. One year we had a great catastrophe. My younger brother Ben had to have an appendectomy, and at the last minute, Mother could not attend the Convention and play the piano for our skit. Miss Evelyn and all the students were in Birmingham, and we didn't have the music! Besides, even if we had music, who would play it? Mrs. Sara Folmar, the science teacher and mother of our classmate June, drove to Birmingham with the music and saved the day.

Who would play the music? Everyone decided I, Nancy Williams, was to be the pianist for our skit. Oh, no! My heart skipped several beats. I played the music at home all the time, but was I sufficiently prepared? Besides that, I had the finale solo, "Somebody Bigger than You and I," and how could I sing it and play for myself? Fortunately, Nelda Ann Moore (Bell) was part of our program, and she played the piano well. She could accompany me. When the time came, I slid off the piano bench, and Nelda Ann slid on. The show must go on! All did their parts well, including my boyfriend Curtis, who had a leading part. Once again, the judges announced Luverne High School to be the winner!

Throughout the school year, there were programs and skits of all kinds. If Mother wasn't playing the piano, I was. Mickey Smith and I were voted "Most Talented" in the Who's Who contest in 1956. One time, Mother and Miss Evelyn dolled me up in Mother's long evening dress and coached me to sing "St. Louis Blues" in a low, throaty voice. The teal-colored dress with rhinestones on the shoulders had a slit up the side, and I wore dark makeup with bright red

Mickey Smith and Nancy, voted Most Talented in Who's Who at Luverne High School, 1956

lipstick and a beauty mole penciled beside my mouth! I can't remember how that fit into the program, but I was only too happy to "ham it up." It's hard to believe this "good little girl" could portray such a worldly woman, but acting was great fun then and now. (See Chapter 36 for my Minnie Pearl skits.)

During the fall seasons when I was a cheerleader at Luverne High, I got so hoarse I could hardly talk, much less sing. However, I continued to go to my voice lessons with Miss Ethel in the block building next to the football field. Friday nights at the football games were thrilling times, especially

Curtis Petrey, halfback for LHS Tigers, 1956-57

Nancy, head cheerleader at LHS, 1956-57

when we ran on the field at the end. I was always looking for Curtis, number 23, and his good, sweaty hug!

In the eighth grade Miss Ethel offered to give me free voice lessons, as long as I would come to her studio to play the piano accompaniments for her other voice students. I was happy to do it, and I enjoyed learning all the pieces for this "job." Accompanying is a skill all its own, and Miss Ethel taught me well how to follow, and not lead, the singer. Miss Ethel comes to my mind today as I employ the accompanying skills she taught me.

I did have one gripe about my voice lessons. Miss Ethel would fall asleep during many of the lessons! I began to feel that she wasn't carrying out her part of the bargain for my free services. I don't remember who accompanied **me**, whether it was Miss Ethel or me. It must have been myself because I can still picture Miss Ethel in her chair beside the piano dozing off! I told Mother about it, and she took action. Miss Ethel was invited to our house. The three of us sat in the living room and talked about the problem. I was relieved that the conversation went well, and Miss Ethel agreed to stop falling asleep! I believe she kept her word.

One of the highlights of my piano study with Miss Ethel was playing duets with my brother, David. Miss Ethel chose two flamboyant pieces, too hard for us, but we mastered them. That was one of her greatest strengths as a teacher, challenging her students to push hard and do the impossible. "Hungarian Rhapsody No. 2" by Franz Liszt and "Malaguena" by Ernesco Lecuona were the two pieces. David had the Secondo (bass) part, and I had the Primo (treble) part in both. To this day it thrills me to think of that exuberant, exotic Liszt piece that required my fingers to fly up and down the keyboard at breakneck speed. It was great fun. The only downside was when I had to sit so close to David on the piano bench after he had come straight from a sweaty football practice!

I greatly desired to keep "Hungarian Rhapsody" in my repertoire, but David wouldn't cooperate. As the saying goes, "If you don't use it, you lose it." I guess God didn't motivate David to practice like He motivated me. Nevertheless, David would try his hand at it

Nancy and brother David, playing "Hungarian Rhapsody No. 2" by Liszt, 1985

from time to time. We succeeded, somewhat, at his house in Huntsville for Thanksgiving in 1985. It is on my bucket list to once more play that beautiful duet with someone!

David and I both had a brief stint with the Luverne High School Band. That was before he played football and before I was a cheerleader. David played the alto horn, and I played the xylophone. I remember the embarrassing incident that curtailed my band involvement. It was my first and last time to march in uniform on the football field. The band went **one** way, and with my head down, concentrating on hitting the right bars of the xylophone, I went the **other** way! I am proud to say that where I failed, several of my grandchildren have succeeded in the band. My son Jim's daughter Taylor played clarinet, and Hannah, played French horn. His youngest, Madeline, is now playing the saxophone. My daughter Susan's son, Zachary Zwerg, played French horn in the band. Although not involved in school bands, Perry's children excelled in playing musical instruments, especially in ministry inside and outside the church. My youngest son Bert developed unusual skill on the guitar. (See Chapter 40 for more of my grandchildren's musical accomplishments.)

# CHAPTER 7

## MY FLAME, MY STEADY, AND MY CO-STAR

Now this part of my story is like "true confessions," and it involves my first kiss! As I said, I developed skill in accompanying, so Miss Ethel asked me to come to Benny Dempsey's voice lessons and accompany him on the piano. Well, not only did I accompany him on the piano, but he picked me up at my house, and I accompanied him in his red jalopy to the studio! He was from Brantley, about ten miles from Luverne, so his lessons were after school hours. In fact, it was almost dark when he drove me back home after his lessons. After doing this "job" for quite some time, the inevitable kiss transpired! It was not inside, but outside the jalopy, so this account is G-rated. Ha!

Benny had a beautiful baritone voice, and Miss Ethel gave him some all-time favorite classics to sing – "Ol' Man River," "On the Road to Mandalay," "Without a Song," "I'll Walk with God," and "The Lord's Prayer." One Sunday afternoon I went with him to Brantley to play "The Lord's Prayer" for him in a program. When it was over, I felt uneasy. There was a big question mark in my mind – had I skipped a whole section? Being around that tall, handsome boy must have thrown me! At first, I wondered why a future football star for Bear Bryant at the University of Alabama would give me the time of day. But later I discovered that he had a weakness for girls, lots of them, and not just for me. In my mind, he was a short-term "flame," not steady boyfriend material. I would enjoy his attention the brief time that it lasted, I decided. Anyway, my love affair with Curtis came before and continued long after my tenth- and eleventh-grade romance with Benny Dempsey. The gorgeous music Benny sang added to my infatuation, but I soon discovered that I could spend a lifetime with Curtis Petrey.

Curtis and I were given the opportunity to take ballroom dancing. Our parents paid the bill, and we drove to Lapine, just up the road from Petrey, to take lessons with other teenagers in the old Community Center. Our instructor was Bobby Davis, who had a dance studio in Montgomery. We learned the fox trot-box step, the rhumba, samba, tango, and waltz! Those were fun times. Curtis did not come from a musical family like I did. He was a great athlete, but dancing was not his thing. I'm not sure he ever mastered the two-step, but we persevered, and it was well worth the time to have his arms around me.

After many musical skits "under my belt," I was ready for the big time. Mrs. Evelyn Turner was famous for her Senior Plays, and many times she chose a musical. Her choice for our class of 1957 was *The Desert Song.* It was an operetta with music by Sigmund Romberg and book and lyrics by Oscar Hammerstein II, Otto Harbach and Frank Mandel. With Miss Evelyn as the Director and my mother as the pianist, it would be a first-class production. The tale was inspired by the 1925 uprising of the Riffs, a group of Moroccan fighters, against French colonial rule.

Here is the plot: the hero, Pierre Birabeau, adopts a mild-mannered disguise to keep his true identity as the Red Shadow a secret. He loves a beautiful and spirited French girl, Margot Bonvalet, who loves his hero persona but does not know his real personality, which he keeps hidden under a milquetoast persona. I was overjoyed to receive the leading role of Margot. Curtis would be cast as Captain Paul Fontaine. June Folmar was cast as Azuri, the dancing girl who knows the true identity of the Red Shadow and tries to attract Captain Fontaine. Jack Thomas, a fellow cheerleader and a good singer, got the leading role of the Red Shadow/Pierre Birabeau.

During rehearsals I did not like seeing Curtis and June in a romantic scene. I wondered what Curtis thought about me with Jackie. Singing the beautiful songs of the musical was the most fulfilling part of the play, so I kept my mind on doing the best I could. It did worry me, however, that in one scene I would have to kiss the Red Shadow on the lips! Jackie and I had always been good friends, fellow cheerleaders, but there was no romantic chemistry between us.

One day, Miss Evelyn, Jackie, and I, just the three of us, were in a school room rehearsing "the kiss." Jackie and I faced each other from across the room, and Jackie began to move toward me, his expression of desire increasing. I stood there like a statue, dreading his approach. Mustering up all my courage, I was ready to make the sacrifice for the sake of art. Jackie was now right in my face, but his lips were quivering! I could not hold back the laughter, and Miss Evelyn was disappointed. She said we must get it right, and we tried several times more. Alas! No success.

The night of the production I didn't know how it would come out. The script called for the Red Shadow to passionately grab Margot, his red cape encompassing them, and hold her in a deep kiss. This was a key part of the play. What did I do? Well, I guess it may have been funny to the audience because our lips "missed" each other! The photo in our yearbook betrayed our "near-miss kiss!"

I would like to think that the torn picture was the result of Curtis' jealousy!

Hopefully, the beautiful music redeemed the lack of acting skills.

> *Blue heaven and*
> *you and I*
> *And sand kissing a*
> *moonlit sky,*
> *A desert breeze*
> *whispering a lul-*
> *laby.*

The Red Shadow (Jack Thomas) and Margot (Nancy) in *The Desert Song*, LHS Senior play, 1957

*Only stars above you to see I love you.*
*Oh! Give me that night divine,*
*And let my arms in yours entwine.*
*The Desert Song calling, its voice enthralling*
*Will make you mine!*
*(Margot and the Red Shadow kiss!)*[5]

Graduation from Luverne High School was a bittersweet experience. It was sad to think that our classmates would be going separate ways, and some of us may never see each other again. The solo I sang for graduation was certainly appropriate, "My Friend," by Albert Hay Malotte. The song ended thus: "... *Tho' time may part the paths we wander, this feeling still will remain; and when at last we go unto our journey's end, we'll meet again, my friend.*"

Nancy singing "My Friend" at LHS graduation, 1957

5    *The Desert Song*, a musical play in two acts (New York: Samuel French, 1932), p. 60. It was made into a movie in 1943 and 1953.

# CHAPTER 8

## IN THE LORD'S HOUSE

I was only in the eighth grade, but the Lord was ready for me to use my abilities for Him in His house with His people. I aspired to be the pianist for my Youth Sunday School Department at Luverne Methodist Church. One of my heroes was Lilellen Hicks, and she had been filling that post. When she moved up to a higher class, I eagerly assumed her position. We sang from the Cokesbury Hymnal in our assembly before we broke up into separate classes. I soon was able to play most of the hymns. We wore out hymns like "Give of Your Best to the Master." The words were just right for our age, and they lodged in my heart:

> Give of your best to the Master; Give of the strength of your youth;
> Throw your soul's fresh, glowing ardor into the battle for truth.
> Jesus has set the example; Dauntless was He, young and brave;
> Give Him your loyal devotion, Give Him the best that you have.
> Give of your best to the Master; Give of the strength of your youth;
> Clad in salvation's full armor, Join in the battle for truth.[6]

I was also the pianist for MYF (Methodist Youth Fellowship) which met on Sunday nights in the Ben Bricken Room. The evening service that followed upstairs in the sanctuary always had the choir loft full of young people. It made us feel special to be the Sunday night choir. A few of the youth, including me, sang in the adult choir on Sunday mornings. I remember that Mother warned me not to be persuaded to sing the alto part because it

---

6    Mrs. Charles Barnard, "Give of Your Best to the Master," # 187, *The Cokesbury Worship Hymnal*, C.A. Bowen, D.D., Gen. Ed. (Abingdon-Cokesbury Press: Nashville).

would limit my vocal range. Maybe she aspired for me to become a coloratura soprano! She knew that because of my ability to read music, the choir director would try to assign me the alto part. I am glad I obeyed my mother because my vocal range did develop in the higher register and gave me much more versatility in solos. I sang the Second Soprano part on occasion, which really fit my voice quality the best, but it was greater fun to hit the high notes. (In the 1980s I even hit a high C. However, in one performance I opened my mouth for that C, and nothing came out! I was greatly embarrassed.)

In my last years of high school, I developed another musical skill, playing the pipe organ. Mrs. Ida Hicks, Lilellen's mother, was gracious enough to teach a few of us how to play the organ. The finger technique was different from playing the piano. You had to maneuver your fingers from key to key to connect the notes, so the music flowed in a sustained manner. (The organ has no sustaining, or damper, pedal to help you connect, as the piano has.) There were two keyboards on this organ for different functions. Sometimes your right hand played the upper manual, called the Swell, and your left hand played the lower manual, the Great, or vice versa. For the most grandiose sound, you played the Great manual with both hands and all the stops pulled out! There were all kinds of sounds for various types of music, and the appropriate stops had to be pulled out. This was quite tricky, and usually there was no time to spare, as the different sections of a piece called for different combinations of stops. This was hard enough, but the foot pedals were murder! Playing the pedals required lots of practice. Your feet had to feel their way around. Toes and heels were used. It was best to wear shoes that had thin soles and flexibility. There was no time to look down at your feet, so you prayed you would hit the right pedals! There was also a volume pedal to deal with. How did I ever learn? I wish I could say I mastered it, but I did not.

Throughout my life there were opportunities to play the organ, including the electric kind. An organ has greater versatility than a piano, but the piano was always my favorite instrument. I filled in for the organist a few times at St. Luke United Methodist Church in Tupelo in the late 1960s and 1970s. After God called my husband Curtis into full-time ministry in 1976, he was appointed to a church with an organ in Potts Camp, Mississippi. I played that organ, and the people really enjoyed the music. When Curtis retired, and we moved home, I played the organ at Luverne United Methodist Church on occasion. Miss Ida's granddaughter and Lilellen's daughter, Stephanie Jones, was the organist and a superb one. She showed me the ropes. There I was, back at the organ I had first learned to play on. I still believed nothing was more beautiful than piano music, but certainly the organ played at full volume can "shake the rafters" and evoke rapturous praise from the worshipers of God.

# CHAPTER 9

## HUNTINGDON COLLEGE

How well I remember the day when my mother sat down with me and some of her friends at Rogers Drug Store in the heart of Luverne and talked about my going to college. Mother had attended Woman's College in Montgomery, and she and Daddy were sending me there. It was now Huntingdon College. At the time I did not realize how fortunate I was because most likely the tuition of this private, Methodist-affiliated college was high. Mother said I must get a teacher's license, for it would serve as a kind of insurance in my life. Being a teacher would assure me of a good, steady-paying job, in case my future husband needed help in supporting us. Mother had been teaching for quite some time at that point, and her salary was needed for our family of five. I could see the logic of that, and I agreed.

At Huntingdon I selected speech as my major, but I also took piano lessons from Miss Virginia Stiles. My speech classes were interesting and enjoyable. However, Miss Stiles thought I had selected the wrong major. She called Mother and me into her studio and insisted that I change my major to music, that I was talented and needed to develop that talent. We both could see that she was probably right, so I changed my major to music. I don't have any other memories of Miss Stiles, but I am grateful she helped set me on the right course.

I do have memories of Dr. Harald Rohlig, who taught organ mainly, but also piano, at Huntingdon College for more than 50 years. He is esteemed by them as a music legend. His greatness did not escape me when I was there in 1957-58. Just recently, I learned about his background and can now appreciate more than ever how blessed I was to know him.

> Harald Rohlig (1926-2014). As the son of a Methodist clergyman who opposed Hitler's regime, Rohlig was forced to join the Hitler Youth at the age of 10 when his family's food and basic necessities were restricted. His father was later incarcerated at the Bergen-Belsen concentration camp. In 1943, Rohlig was drafted into the Luftwaffe. Before World War II ended he was captured by American soldiers, from whom he received good treatment, and spent three years in a French prison camp.
>
> After his release from the prison camp in 1948, Rohlig returned to his musical studies. A musical prodigy who was composing and concertizing before he was in his teens, Rohlig studied at the Royal Academy of Music in London and earned his doctorate in pipe organ design from Osnabruck Conservatory.
>
> In 1953, he immigrated with his wife to Linden, Alabama, where he taught piano and organ, played the organ, and conducted choirs at the Methodist and Baptist churches. He moved to Montgomery, Alabama, in 1955 to take a faculty position at Huntingdon College, retiring in 2006. During his career he wrote over 1,000 pieces of music and published over 300 works. His legacy includes design of several neo-Baroque pipe organs in the Southeast, including one in Tuscaloosa, Alabama.[7]

He had an adorable German accent and a kind demeanor. I used to sneak into his studio, when the campus was quiet, to practice on his grand piano. I was not even a student of his, but the practice rooms had those old uprights, and they were uninspiring. One day he caught me! I was very apologetic, but he didn't seem to mind that I was there. During our conversation he told me something very interesting:

The German composer Robert Schumann could not work out why he (and everyone else) had trouble lifting up the fourth

---

7   https://en.wikipedia.org/wiki/Harald_Rohlig

finger on each hand. The truth is that the fourth finger is lacking a tendon which the other fingers have, allowing them to be lifted independently of the other fingers. To this end Schumann had a special contraption constructed which would pull his fourth finger back a little further each day in order to strengthen it. The result however was catastrophic, as he snapped the only tendon for that finger and lost use of it completely.[8]

Our conversation was special, but he did something that had a much greater impact on me. I was a part of the choir Dr. Rohlig directed to present the well-loved *Messiah* by George Frederic Handel. Our rehearsals took place in the choir loft of St. John's Episcopal Church. **This was my first time to sing the *Messiah*, and I loved it. Singing nothing but Scripture is unique because God's Word becomes embedded in your mind and emotions.**

I will never forget the pathos of the Suffering Servant passage of Isaiah 53, all because of the way Dr. Rohlig demonstrated how we should sing it, especially these words from verses 4-5: *"SURELY, SURELY! He has borne our GRIEFS! And carried our SORROWS! ... But He was WOUNDED for our transgressions; He was BRUISED for our iniquities ...."* Dr. Rohlig mustered all the strength he had to passionately sing the two words, **"Surely, surely,"** at the greatest volume possible, directing the orchestra with his baton as a weapon! He drew the same pathos out of us singers that was inside himself. What got inside me more were the words and music to **"wounded"** and **"bruised."** Handel had composed the music in such a way as to **stretch** the stringed instruments and voices with a tormenting sound, mimicking the **excruciating pain** of our Lord and Savior Jesus Christ as He hung on the cross!

I didn't know it at the time, but I realize now that Dr. Rohlig's background under Hitler's regime, being a prisoner of war, and his father being in a concentration camp gave him a "fellowship of suffering" with Jesus, hence his depth of feeling for the musical description of the crucifixion. Through my brief association with

---

8    Piano Learners, "Piano Finger Exercises," June 16, 2012, http://www. pianolearners.com/

Dr. Harald Rohlig, I was spiritually and musically enriched. I know it was **no coincidence** that he came to Huntingdon in 1955, and I came in 1957. It was **part of God's plan for my life** that I learn from this outstanding musician and man of faith.

# CHAPTER 10

## UNIVERSITY OF ALABAMA

Before I transferred to the University of Alabama in the fall of 1958, my mother decided I should enter the Miss Alabama pageant in Birmingham. We would stay in the home of Aunt Belle and Uncle Buddy Hudson who had moved there from Luverne. Aunt Belle was my daddy's sister, and they had lived next door to my paternal grandmother, "Big Mama," Della Williams. Growing up, David and I had great fun playing with Aunt Belle and Uncle Buddy's son Willie, our first cousin. His sister Gloria was grown up from our perspective, so we didn't "play" with her. However, I did stand in awe of how beautifully she could sing. She was a voice student of Miss Ethel before my time.

Being in the State Pageant for Miss America was an experience I was not especially proud of, although I made it to the semi-finals. I have no idea how I was rated in the interview portion, but I didn't think I rated well in the talent portion. I chose a flashy and difficult piano piece, "Revolutionary Etude" by Frederic Chopin, and I made an obvious stumble. I don't remember finishing it! This was an embarrassing moment, but at least it was over. I was scared out of my wits and had insomnia the night before. Now we could return home, and I could get ready for the big University, which would be another frightening experience for a small-town girl.

After going through Rush and being accepted into the Alpha Gamma Delta Sorority, I settled down to dormitory life. Unfortunately, I had insomnia almost nightly for the first few weeks, which led to a visit to the infirmary. Changing dorms and getting a single room helped greatly. Also, seeing my high school sweetheart Curtis on campus was reassuring, and we resumed our steady relationship.

I liked all my music courses, except the theory course under Dr. Frederic Goossen. It was hard because this was an area of ignorance in my prior musical education. I made all As and Bs in college, except for a C in Dr. Goossen's class. Learning chord progressions was brand new for me, and I never mastered it. Some things have stayed with me, however, and my skill in piano playing was helped by the textbook for this course.

Miss Margaret Christy taught me sight singing, using numbers for the notes of the scale, not syllables (do-re-mi-fa-so-la-ti-do). Miss Christy was the cellist in the famed Čadek String Quartet, which was founded by Ottokar Čadek in 1946. In 1955, the recital hall at the University of Alabama's newly built Music and Speech Building was named Čadek Hall. That is where my music classes were held and where I gave my senior recital. Miss Christy also taught cello, and I learned the difficult accompaniment music for some of her students. The **skill of sight-singing** that I developed in her class was very valuable, and I have used it ever since. I am grateful for Miss Christy.

Dr. Fred Hyde taught me Music Appreciation. I made an A in his class by studying the text book thoroughly for every test. I actually didn't learn anything from Dr. Hyde because I slept through every class! It was scheduled right after lunch, so my "absence" was not Dr. Hyde's fault. His voice, however, did contribute to my drowsiness.

My voice teacher was a man, Sanford A. Linscome, which was a new experience for me. It was during my time with him that I finally learned the correct way to breathe and produce a pure tone. All my life my tone had been "breathy," but when I learned to breathe from the diaphragm and regulate the amount of breath for the tones, my voice strengthened. I could sing pure tones with greater volume. The best thing of all was there was no fatigue, and my enjoyment was heightened. One day it all "clicked."

In high school Miss Ethel had given me some beautiful voice pieces, including "One Fine Day," an aria from the opera, *Madame Butterfly* by Puccini. I could appreciate some of the arias from various operas, but I had never appreciated opera in general. I preferred Broadway musicals, where the dialogue is spoken, not sung, as it is in opera. It always seemed ridiculous to me that the dialogue was sung, and I hated the wide vibrato in an operatic voice. However, I must admit that I fell in love with the Italian pieces that Dr. Linscome introduced me to. I could see how these numbers were composed in such a way in the Italian language as to bring out the most melodious tones imaginable. My favorites were "Caro mio ben" by Giordani and "Se tu m'ami, se sospiri" by Pergolesi. Oh, how much fun it was to sing these and other pieces like them, but that was the extent of my affinity for "operatic singing."

Wedding of Curtis and Nancy at Luverne Methodist Church - September 3, 1959

Curtis and I got married on September 3, 1959, right before we entered our junior year at the University. No one told Curtis what patience he would have to develop to live with a music major, although he had a taste of the stringent requirements through his attendance with me at the concerts on campus. He loved to tell the story of a particular concert in which we were bored to tears. The music faculty had selected the pieces played by the guest orchestra. We found this out at the conclusion of the program, when the conductor turned toward the audience and said, "I was surprised at the pieces the faculty selected, which were not only very difficult to play but also were not concert favorites in my experience. Thank you for your patience, but now you can sit back and relax. We are going to play 'Turkey in the Straw!'" Needless to say, the audience went wild, and Curtis was glad the music faculty got their come-uppance! Ha!

The requirements for a bachelor's degree in Music Education included four semesters learning to play an instrument in each of the four families of instruments – strings, woodwinds, brass, and percussion. Poor Curtis had to endure my practice times on the trumpet, flute, violin, and drum pad. I excelled in drumming. Dr. Ed Cleino was a good percussion teacher. With the drumsticks I could beat out almost any rhythm with a minimum of practice. Because of the teaching of Miss Christy and Dr. Cleino, I had already had the practice of sight reading intricate rhythms, and it was great fun. The Lord was merciful to Curtis that I never played an actual drum!

Miss Christy was also my strings teacher. I could quickly see why the violin took years and years of study to go from squeaky to smooth and beautiful. In that one semester I did master "Twinkle, Twinkle, Little Star." I can well remember practicing it in our first apartment at 3A Terrace Court in Tuscaloosa. We had a living room, a bathroom, a bedroom, a kitchen, and a tiny hallway in the middle. It was in this hallway that I drew the bow over the strings, causing excruciating pain for all in hearing distance, especially my new husband! He decided to keep me anyway.

In our second apartment, D-12C Northington campus, we had a rental piano moved in, which was the ultimate test for Curtis' patience! Not only would he have to endure that test, but another test was the lungs of our first baby, Perry Lee Petrey, born on July 30, 1960. Now Perry's cries would compete with the musical cacophony of the piano for another year at the University. Our proud father and husband passed the test.

What an honor it was to have Colonel Carleton Butler, the Director of the Alabama Million Dollar Band for three courses. The woodwind instrument he chose for me was the flute, for which he said I had the perfect embouchure (shape of the lips to fit the mouthpiece). It is a beautiful instrument, but it would receive great abuse at my hands. Curtis enjoyed describing my flute practice. I would sit on the bed, position the flute perfectly to my mouth, have my fingers at the ready for the notes, and then blow across the mouthpiece as Colonel Butler taught me. However, no sound came out! I would blow again and no sound. Then I would continue to blow, blow, blow, and no sound would emerge except the increasingly forceful breaths. Then I would cry and cry and cry. Drying my eyes, I would try again, still with little to no success. Somehow, I finished the course. I think I even made an A, which must have been for effort, not actual playing!

In contrast to the flute, the trumpet was much easier to play. Evidently, my embouchure was perfect for the trumpet, not the flute. To this day I am pretty good at blowing a horn. I can make several different sounds on the shofar (ram's horn). The third course Colonel Butler taught me was choral conducting. The degree I was pursuing was in choral music, not band music. He was surprised when I sang while conducting, but it seemed the natural thing to do. The right hand doing the different directing patterns for different time signatures (4/4, 3/4, 2/4, 6/8) was "a piece of cake." The hardest part was the use of the left hand, signaling changes in volume and entrances for different parts (soprano, alto, tenor, bass). I didn't quite master it, but I made an A in the course. Conducting skill would come in handy in my future endeavors, directing school and church choirs.

Another faculty member at the University who taught me a lot about choral music was Dr. Roland Johnson. It was a big blessing to sing in the University Choral Union under his direction. He played violin and conducted the orchestra also. He and Miss Christy were in the University String Quartet which traveled all over the nation to perform. God gave me the very best music educators, for which I am so grateful.

# CHAPTER 11

## PIANO TECHNIQUE WITH MRS. PENICK

The music teacher at the University who had the greatest and most life-changing impact on me was my piano teacher, Mrs. Amanda Penick. At the time I did not realize that the Lord had chosen for me the very best piano teacher "in the world." It was only after reading of her death (2016) that I realized this awesome fact. [9] She was even like a mentor to me in my personal life. I was only 20 and needed some guidance as a young wife. One day when I came into her studio wearing maternity clothes, she began acting like a mother hen. She recommended a friend of hers, Dr. David Partlow, as the obstetrician I needed to deliver my baby. I followed up on her advice, and he was the doctor who delivered Perry in the Druid City Hospital in Tuscaloosa.

Our relationship had both a positive and a negative side. Mrs. Penick was determined that I learn a special technique she taught all her students, the "accent method." It was a long and laborious exercise, and I hated it! Hadn't I been playing the piano for over 13 years already? Did I need this "accent method"? It really caused tension between us, and one day she "kicked me out" of her studio! Of course, I went back, and I was more docile and continued to learn the "accent method." It began with "ones," which meant accenting each single note. The process was thus: fingers rested curved and

---

9    Amanda Penick taught at the University of Alabama for 61 years and was the longest-tenured faculty member in the State of Alabama! Read about her unparalleled career in performing and teaching piano: http://www.tuscaloosanews.com/news/20160620/longtime-university-of-alabama-music-teacher-dies

relaxed on the keys, then suddenly the thumb forcefully pushed down the note by the weight of the wrist going down. Then I had to wait for all the tension to drain out of my hand. Next, the wrist raised the hand, fingers level to the keyboard and still touching the keys, and the process began again with the next note. After perfecting the "ones," I stepped up to "twos" – the thumb accented the first note, wrist going down, tension draining out, then the whole hand lifted up with the index finger lightly playing, but not accenting, the second note on the way up. It was a glory day when I got through with ones, twos, threes, and fours!

So, what was the outcome of learning the "accent method"? I could then play runs effortlessly for a very long time and never get tired. For the first time in over 13 years, my fingers were curved and relaxed on the keys, and my enjoyment increased 100-fold! Mrs. Penick now had a new challenge for me, the principle of the "dying tone." That sounded funny to me, but it was an ingenious method of connecting the tones in a more expressive way than I had ever done before. I had assumed I always listened carefully as I played, but how wrong I was. I was not listening at all, until I began implementing the principle of the "dying tone." There again, Mrs. Penick knew best. Her techniques increased my enjoyment and skill in piano playing. My gratitude to her knew no bounds. Her teaching changed my life!

Mrs. Penick would often say to me at my lessons, "We have been talking about you in faculty meetings." Then she would urge me to change my course of study from a Bachelor of Science degree in Music Education to a Bachelor of Music degree in Arts and Sciences. There were two reasons I would not even consider it. First, my mother had insisted I must get a teacher's certificate as a kind of financial insurance, and that would not be acquired with a music degree in Arts and Sciences. Music students getting those degrees would most likely end up being piano teachers, with a few being concert pianists. That did not appeal to me, although I taught my own four children piano lessons for a while plus a few more students over the years, both young and old. The second reason was that B.M. students were required to practice four hours a day! With a B.S. degree program, I was required to practice one hour a day. Honestly, I did not fulfill even that minimum requirement. Being cooped up in a small practice room with my only companion a piano for a full hour daily was not even **having** a life, in my opinion. Nevertheless, I was complimented that the music faculty was impressed with my talent. It was a gift from God, so I would not dare to brag.

The Lord has a way of keeping us dependent on Him and curbing our egotistic bent. Mrs. Penick put me on the University's public television program. Dr. Frederic Goossen was host. My mother called everyone in Luverne to watch the program. To say I was nervous was putting it mildly. The first memorized piece Mrs. Penick selected for me was "Sonata No. 7 in D Major, Op. 10, No. 3, Presto movement," by Ludwig van Beethoven. It was seven pages long, in the middle of Book I of Beethoven Sonatas, which was 341 pages long, and my parents had to buy the book for that **one** Sonata! What a long title this piece had. I wished it had a nickname, such as "Revolutionary Etude" by Chopin. Unlike Miss Ethel, it was typical of Mrs. Penick to assign piano compositions that were not familiar to the average person. Still, I came to appreciate these lesser known pieces she gave me, and I'm sure she was attempting to develop some area of skill in my playing with each piece. As for me, I just wanted to play pretty and exciting stuff.

The second piece I was to play was also not well-known except in university circles, I would imagine – the second of three suites, "Sonetto 104 del Petrarca," (Sonnet of Petrach) from *Annees de pelerinage* (Years of Pilgrimage) by Franz Liszt. This piano piece described Liszt's travels in Italy. Whereas the Beethoven piece was militaristic-sounding, this one was romantic, which I liked better.

I played the Beethoven Sonata just fine, until I got to a bridge part in the middle. I stumbled and couldn't remember how to go on. Usually, when this happened, I would go back to the first and begin again, but I began to picture myself, returning over and over to the first and not being able to get past the bridge. That thought horrified me, and my fingers froze on the keys! I probably did not even end it on a D chord. The camera moved away from me, and Dr. Goossen came hurrying over to ask if I would like to use the sheet music for my second number. For some reason, a brave resolve gripped me, and I said to Dr. Goossen that I would play the second number by memory just as I planned. What a relief when I finished the Liszt piece without a major mistake!

I could hardly wait to get back to the apartment to see what Curtis would say. Had he noticed that I stopped in the middle of the Beethoven Sonata? Did he think everyone noticed or only a few people? How did he evaluate my performance? My face fell when Curtis, with no musical education, said he could tell when I stopped in the middle! Next, I had to know what Mother thought.

Mother called and said her phone was ringing off the hook with friends calling to say how much they enjoyed my playing. The next time I was home, Uncle Crook was at the house, and he commented on my performance. He really liked it, but he added, "That first number sure did leave me hanging though." His was a kind but accurate evaluation, and I continued to be humbled. God couldn't let the intoxication of being on television spoil me.

Recently, I talked about this television appearance with my younger brother Ben, and he remembered it well. He was probably 13 years old at the time. Ben said he thought it was great. He said that Mother had commented while I was playing, "Just look at that left hand!" I asked him if he noticed that my hands froze on the keys in the first number. He said he didn't notice. Now **that** is the memory I want to keep fresh in my mind.

# Chapter 12

## From College to Career

For a Music Education degree, a student is not required to give a solo recital, but the recital is shared with a student who is earning a music degree in Arts and Sciences. My recital was with Gwen Porter, a soprano, and the program was titled "Junior Recital," although it was my *senior* recital. I only received one hour credit each semester for my piano and voice classes, although I had to practice as if they were three-hour courses. As a Music Education student, I continued to be treated as a "stepchild" up to the very end!

Mrs. Penick accompanied Miss Porter. My piano pieces included the two I had played on television, the Beethoven Sonata and the Liszt piece. Also, I played "Two Sinfonias" by J. S. Bach, "Etude in A flat Major, Op. 25, No. 1" by Chopin, and "Fairy Tale" by Medtner.

All my family drove up to Tuscaloosa for the recital in Čadek Hall, March 24, 1961, and I was thankful for the support. Miss Ethel sent me flowers. My performance was pretty good, as I remember. Unfortunately, as I was playing, the power went off momentarily, and the tape recording lost part of my performance. Still, it was a relief to at last have fulfilled the instrumental part of my course requirements.

The education requirements were climaxed by two semesters of Practice Teaching, one in the elementary school and one in the high school. I was wearing maternity clothes when I walked into the 4th grade classroom at the elementary school adjacent to the U of A campus. The children ducked their heads and giggled! They finally warmed up to me though, and my semester with them yielded an A. Practice Teaching at Tuscaloosa High School was another matter.

The first day I thought, "How in the world can I do this? I have not even been a member of a school chorus, much less directed one!" The students purposely made it hard for me, but, somehow, I received an 'A' for that semester of Practice Teaching also. The Tuscaloosa High Choral Concert was on May 18, 1961, and I directed one number and accompanied one number.

Since I was a married student and getting ready to move with Curtis and little Perry to Montgomery, Alabama, I was too busy to go through the graduation ceremony. What mattered was that I had graduated and had my college diploma. With the coveted teacher's certificate, I would soon make my debut as a teacher of choral music in the public school. The Practice Teaching courses I had at the University in both elementary school and high school were supposed to initiate me as a professional teacher, but they were not adequate on-the-job training. I was about to go through the fire!

We moved into Edgemont Apartments on Edgemont Drive. I had just inherited my grandmother's piano, and we had it moved from Brundidge, Alabama, to our apartment. I felt sorry for the movers. A piano is the heaviest of all furniture, and they had to move it to our upstairs apartment. After a brief stint selling World Book Encyclopedias, Curtis got a job as a cameraman at WSFA-TV but later moved on to the *Montgomery Advertiser* in the ad display department. I applied to the school system for a teaching job in choral music. While waiting for an opening, I got a job at the First National Bank, Cloverdale Branch in Montgomery. We employed a baby sitter for Perry, not much over a year old. It was heart-wrenching to leave my precious baby, listening to his cries as I closed the apartment door. I had no choice but to earn money for our basic needs, and I reported to the Proof Department at the bank. Instead of reading music, I was now "speed-reading" checks for the pockets of the proof machine!

The bank required me to take banking courses, but my musical talents still came in handy. At the A.I.B. (American Institute of Banking) Christmas Breakfast in 1961 and 1962, I was invited to sing. My solos were "Jesus Bambino" and "O Holy Night," accompanied by Jacquelyn Hodges (Earnest), also a student of Miss Ethel's.

Back at the bank, I was promoted to Teller. One day a man came up to my window, introduced himself as the Superintendent of Schools and offered me the position of Choral Teacher with one class of Speech at Capitol Heights Junior High. This position would be open the first day of the second semester, beginning in January 1963. The Superintendent explained that the male choral teacher who taught the first semester had absconded with the funds! There are always fundraisers in school music programs, so it was those funds that he stole. He was promptly fired, and they needed a teacher to fill out the school year.

I was literally scared out of my wits. I had only days to prepare, and I had no idea what I was doing. Added to that, this school was a bigger school than I had ever been in, and these were big city kids. A kind teacher who was right down the hall from me took me under her wing, and I held on for dear life! Besides the actual teaching, there were records to keep, and she was expert in that.

I didn't know what the former teacher had done, so I started from scratch, searching the filing cabinets for music we could use and figuring out my lesson plans. I had to select suitable songs for seventh, eighth, and ninth grade girls. By the time I got this job, Curtis, Perry, and I had moved out of the apartment into a brand new house, but the grand piano would not fit in the living room. I had to get rid of it and buy a new spinet piano, a small one. The money had been provided already because Curtis' daddy, Mr. Loyce, had given us $500 for Christmas. Curtis graciously agreed to spend it on the piano, not a luxury, but a necessity in this teaching job. I went in Mary's House of Music across from the bank and found a Hamilton spinet that cost almost exactly $500. I was set.

Well, here came the students on the first day of the new semester. I put one foot in front of another, played a note on the piano one after the other, and spoke and sang a word, one after another. By the end of the day I had survived the fire! I drove home, looked in the refrigerator, found a beer on the shelf (I never drank a drop before this), drank it all down, got in the bed, got under the covers, and tried to go to sleep and forget everything! I was severely traumatized. Then the next day I got up, drove to school, went through the same activities, and drove back home. I was surviving each day, and after a week, I began to breathe.

It was phenomenal how much I learned in a few weeks. I had always been a pretty good sight reader, but I had never read a choral score of three parts (I Soprano, II Soprano, Alto), playing all notes simultaneously at a glance, listening for the voices on those parts as well as singing with them, and conducting the music with one hand or the other when I could spare it! I would rehearse the girls in various combinations of voice parts, singing with them while playing the parts, one at the time, two at the time, then all three together. I would straighten out rhythmic errors. In addition to that, I would lead them in vocalization and exercises in rhythm. People who are mentally sluggish should take up music! It is hard work but so rewarding.

I sat at the piano during all the teaching until I had to use a student accompanist to prepare for the concerts. I preferred to do it myself. I was earning my pay. But the hardest aspect of teaching was not about music, but about dealing with personalities. One day one of my best singers came in the room unannounced during my free period. She raked me over the coals for not giving her some solo part she felt she deserved. I was shocked. I don't know how the principal found out about it, but he called her into the office, and she paid dearly for her insubordination. I appreciated the help because discipline is never pleasant. A teacher has to keep good order, or there will be no teaching and no learning.

My first challenge was taking the Glee Club to Troy State College for the District Choral Festival on February 21-22, 1963. Our two songs were "Evening Prayer" from *Hansel and Gretel* by Engelbert Humperdinck and "Hallelujah" by Louis Lewandowski. We came home with a Superior rating! To God be the glory.

The next challenge was rehearsing and co-directing a combined girls' choir for the Easter Sunrise Service at Cramton Bowl on April 14, 1963. The Capitol Heights and Goodwin Junior High choirs of 150 girls, 75 from each school, sang "Hallelujah" by Lewandowski and "Jesus, Priceless Treasure" by J. S. Bach.

The final big event of the lone semester I taught at Capi-

## To Sing In Sunrise Service

These members of the Capitol Heights Junior High School Glee Club will be among the 150-voice chorus to sing at the Easter Sunrise Service at Cramton Bowl April 14. From left are Gayle Hamm, Donna Johnson, Judy Hood and Mrs. Nancy Petrey, director.

Nancy's first teaching job - choral director at Capitol Heights Junior High in Montgomery, AL, 1963

tol Heights Junior High was the Spring Concert, "Wonderland." Included in the Seventh Grade Chorus numbers was the French song, "Dites-Moi," from the Rodgers & Hammerstein musical,

*South Pacific.* In the play and movie, little children sing the song in French. The English words are: "Tell me why life is beautiful, tell me why life is gay. Tell me why, dear miss. Is it because you love me?" **I taught it to my two-year-old Perry, and he was such a doll singing it in French!**

*Dites-moi*
*Pourquoi*
*La vie est belle,*
*Dites-moi*
*Pourquoi*
*La vie est gai,*
*Dites-moi*
*Pourquoi,*
*Chere Mad'moiselle,*
*Est-ce que*
*Parce que*
*Vous m'aimez?*

Perry Lee Petrey, two-year-old son of Curtis and Nancy, Montgomery, AL, 1962

This was only **one** song of many in our precocious little boy's repertoire. What a joy he was.

In the concert the Glee Club sang our District Festival songs plus other songs, which included "I Feel Pretty" and "America!" from the Broadway musical and movie, *West Side Story.* I felt inspired to have the girls hold plastic roses for "America!" At the end of the song they threw them up in the air! It was great fun.

The auditorium was packed, and the concert was a huge success. After the applause and the bows, I saw some students coming from the side of the stage toward me, bringing a silver coffee service. They presented it to me with their appreciation for my teaching. I was bowled over! I had no idea at all that they cared that much for me. What started out as a traumatic experience had turned into a big blessing. The initiation into teaching was over. Praise the Lord!

# CHAPTER 13

## SPIRITUAL QUEST BEGINS IN CORINTH

There were two reasons I did not continue teaching at Capitol Heights Junior High School in Montgomery. Our second child, Susan Elizabeth, was on the way and would be born on January 13, 1964. Also, Curtis had received a job promotion from the *Montgomery Advertiser* to the Daily Corinthian newspaper in Corinth, Mississippi, as Advertising Director. We would be moving in October 1963.

In Corinth besides being a mother to Perry and Susan and helping Curtis in business, I was very active in music clubs, singing and playing the piano. This was a cultured little city. Right away I was on the program committee of the Beethoven Club. I also was involved with the Corinth Music Club and participated in National Music Week each year and in the Festival of Sacred Music as a singer and pianist. For one of these programs I sang songs from *Porgy and Bess*. I can remember dressing up as Bess, dark makeup and all, and singing "Summertime." It is a good thing Perry and Susan weren't teenagers at the time. They would have been scandalized!

Nancy singing "Summertime" from "Porgy and Bess" in Corinth, MS, 1965

Curtis and I were active in social and church events, especially through our friends in the First Methodist Church. We lived in Corinth four years, building a new house and a new business after Curtis left the Daily Corinthian. The Heritage House, a furniture and carpet business, opened June 16, 1965. I helped as bookkeeper and saleslady but was relieved when the First Methodist Church offered me a position as youth worker for the summer of 1966. I was not cut out to be in sales or book-keeping. As a matter of fact, I had been praying, "Lord, please get me out of here. My relationship with Curtis is suffering!"

Curtis and Nancy, Grand Opening of Heritage House in Corinth, MS, 1965

The day Brother Al Dickerson came walking in the store and offered me that position, I knew it was an answer to prayer. However, I said to him, "You must give me some books to read. I need to be a 'better Christian' to lead the youth." Brother Dickerson gave me three books, and I devoured them. At this point I began a serious spiritual quest. Curtis was having his own time of searching after our new pastor, Bill Appleby, sent him to a Lay Witness training event. He felt so uncomfortable as the witnesses began greeting each other with a warm hug and saying, "I love you, and God loves you." Curtis was scared he would be called on like the others to stand up and give a witness, a testimony of how Jesus had come into his life. If he was called on, he wouldn't have anything to say! But all that would soon change for both of us.

Curtis sold everything in The Heritage House except the carpet and renamed the business, Carpet Contractors. He began to expand and decided to open another carpet store in Tupelo, Mississippi. We said goodbye to our wonderful church family and moved our family of four to Tupelo on August 30, 1967.

# CHAPTER 14

## LIFE CHANGES IN TUPELO

Before we left Corinth, Rev. Bill Appleby advised us to join St. Luke United Methodist Church in Tupelo. We took his advice and quickly became very active. We got involved with the youth and Sunday School. I immediately joined the choir. We developed close friendships. Curtis was happy running Carpet Contractors.

We moved into a new house on Tyler Street, and I met the choral director of Milam Junior High School who lived right down the street, Jane Wright. She was recovering from pneumonia and needed a replacement for her job, beginning in January. I applied for the job and got it. We had only been living in Tupelo a few months, and now I was facing a teaching challenge similar to the one in Montgomery.

Coming into the classroom in the middle of the year was not easy, especially since Mrs. Wright was so loved by her students, and she was an excellent choral director. Here I was, going through the fire again. However, in only three months hence something would happen to me that would change everything and supply the help I needed to make it through.

It was on March 26-28, 1968, that we had a Lay Witness Mission at our church. Curtis was in charge of it, and it was his idea. This was a weekend of meetings with Christian witnesses, both young and old, from Mississippi, Alabama, and Tennessee, coming to tell their stories about how their lives were changed when they met Jesus Christ. Although Curtis was "Mr. Church" at that time, and I had been immersed in church life from the cradle, neither of us knew Jesus as our personal Lord and Savior. The more testimonies we heard that weekend the more we knew we didn't have what the witnesses had, and we wanted it. At the conclusion of the weekend, on Sunday morning when the invitation was given, Curtis and I braved the embarrassment and went to the altar. As we knelt there we made a total commitment of our lives to Jesus. When we got up from the altar, we were changed, born again! Jesus was now our Savior, and He was also our Lord, our boss. He would be directing our lives, and what a relief. I had not been doing so well, running my life. Weekly home group meetings were set up to help us grow in our faith and witness. Life was filled with excitement and purpose.

My school spring concert in April came only a month after my salvation experience. It was held at the Tupelo Civic Auditorium. The big stage was daunting, but we arose to the task. Many of our songs were written by Rodgers & Hammerstein and included several from the musical, *Cinderella*. The student accompanist, Bill Carroll, was excellent. The last three numbers were sacred songs. It was a beautiful and successful concert, and I gave God the glory.

After the summer I taught another year. It was during this year that I held auditions for Milam Musicmakers, a select group of girls, singing three parts, I Soprano, II Soprano, and Alto. We had a Christmas concert, also held in the Tupelo Civic Auditorium. The Milam Belles and Beaus and the Milam Musicmakers performed. At the insistence of my students one of my own compositions, *Drifting*, was included in the program. The Spring Concert on March 27, 1969, was held in the Milam Junior High Auditorium because the Band shared the program with us. The Combined Chorus and Band ended the program with "This is My Country." Mrs. Martha Hitch, an accomplished pianist, accompanied the chorus in both concerts.

At the end of that school year, 1968-69, I resigned, and my practice teacher, Gigi Franklin, replaced me. My family life and spiritual growth had priority over my music career, so I left the classroom for a season. Perry was going into the fourth grade, and Susan was in kindergarten. We were building a house out in the country, and Curtis' carpet business was booming. Church life took up more of our time, and we also served on Lay Witness teams. We met Millard and Linda Fuller (who would later be the Founders of Habitat for Humanity) and got involved in their ministry. With all this going on, teaching could wait. My life was taken up with family and ministry.

Music was still a very important part of my life, however. I could never resign from it. I knew God was using me in singing and playing the piano, and it was obvious that the Holy Spirit was anointing me. My singing was totally different! "Fill My Cup" by Richard Blanchard was one of my first solos after I gave my heart to Jesus, and I could see how it blessed people. Besides singing solos in church and on Lay Witness Missions, I was a member of the Tupelo Fortnightly Musicale, an ensemble of Christian ladies who performed at various functions.

Fortnightly Musicale in Tupelo, MS 1972 - Jane Wright, Betty Castles, Jere Ann White, me, Ellie Sparks, Linda Napier (Kinsey), Ruth Johnston, Betty Duvall (King)

# CHAPTER 15

## MISSIONARY IN THE CLASSROOM

In the summer of 1970 after my year off from teaching I got a call from the Superintendent of schools to come back to Milam Junior High and take up my old job. Miss Franklin had married and moved away (I played the organ for her wedding in Winter Haven, Florida). We were settled in our new house, and all was quiet on the home front. I prayed a lot about it and finally got an answer from God. He was sending me back as a "missionary," because the schools were being integrated that year. God knew my heart was for reconciliation between the races, and He had a new mission for me the next two years at Milam, a musical one.

I decided to attend the Fred Waring Choral Workshop in Water Gap, Pennsylvania, in August to thoroughly prepare myself for a challenging teaching assignment. Flying there, meeting choral directors, and meeting the famous Fred Waring, who was dubbed "America's Singing Master," was more than exciting. The most inspiring and helpful thing of all was singing along with all the expert singers on piece after piece after piece of choral music. It was sheer heaven. I also learned something brand new, the handbells.

At break time I couldn't resist going to the grand piano and playing one of the octavos, "O Happy Day." It was fun to play that jazzy arrangement. Later, I was approached about staying on to be the accompanist for the next workshop. What a compliment. I assumed they had heard me playing the piano. My ego was stroked, but I had to decline. Curtis, Perry, and Susan were back home waiting for me, and my family had to come first.

I was so pumped up from my experience at the choral workshop (a stellar vacation), that shortly after returning home I began planning the music for the upcoming school term, 1970-71, and I bought a large reel to reel tape player. Going into the new school year, I was armed and ready. Not long after school started I asked the shop teacher to build some risers for us, and he was happy to do so. I decorated my room and plunged in with vigor, teaching both boys and girls in Eighth and Ninth Grade Chorus and Seventh Grade General Music. I would have a total of 200 chorus students, and I would teach every seventh grader in the school. What an opportunity!

My drive to school each morning from our country home close to the Pontotoc County Line Road, covered quite a few miles, and I used the time mostly to pray that God would use me for His purposes and His glory. I knew I had to live out my faith in the classroom, so that in my speech, music selections, and interaction with the students, Jesus could be seen.

I was not a "politically correct" teacher, you might say. One day in the middle of class, I got a note from the principal that I should no longer discuss "religion" in class. In my office off the classroom, however, I did occasionally have a discreet and brief "counseling" session with a student. One student told me that when she was reading her Bible in study hall, the teacher made her close it and told her not to bring her Bible to school anymore. Before-school devotions were allowed, however. One morning in the auditorium I led the devotional time, and a girl was saved! It was an exciting time to be teaching young, impressionable minds. To this day I am friends with a woman who was in one of my classes at that time, Judith Jones (Long). Through the witness of my practice teacher, Shirley Page (Dillard), she was saved. The Lord used me to help Judith grow in her faith. I felt honored to play a part in helping develop a beautiful servant of God. My light was shining in the classroom.

I believe that the Lord used me to smooth out the integration problems in our school. It was the first time I had taught blacks, and I went out of my way to make them feel accepted and valued. It so happened that there were some outstanding black students in my classes and some good singers. A few had bad attitudes, but Walter was a shining star. Not only did he make good grades and have a beautiful bass voice, but he was very polite and friendly. People like Walter made all the hard work worth it.

Unfortunately, the worst experience I had in my years in the classroom happened at our first concert that term. It took place in the Milam auditorium. The students sang very well, but there was a near-riot in the auditorium during the intermission! My husband helped to bring order. That wasn't the worst thing. After the concert I had a little party in my upstairs classroom. Some of the non-chorus students – probably those rioting at intermission – decided to come get free refreshments. Passing the girls on the stairs, they made obscene advances! I was devastated when I heard about it.

The next day in the classes, I asked the students to write out their evaluations of the concert. Walter wrote, "The singing was great. The audience was the worst thing. Mr. Petrey tried with all his heart to break some of the noise ... I love you, Mrs. Petrey, and I don't like to see you hurt. I also love Curtis." Almost every girl wrote, "Don't blame yourself, Mrs. Petrey. It wasn't your fault." One girl wrote that she had already been harassed like that during the year. Still, I felt awful about it. The many reassurances from my students did help to ease the pain though.

Curtis and I along with others started a Christian non-profit coffee house in downtown Tupelo before the end of the school year. It opened on April 30, 1971, as "One Way Ltd." The purpose was to reach young people for Christ and to give them a place to talk over their troubles. The activities included singing, sharing, praying, study, and recreation. Many of my students attended, and Curtis, I, and our friends were on hand to lend a listening ear, to pray, or to teach.

With family, school, and the coffee house, I had a lot of irons in the fire that spring. Martha Hitch, who had been our accompanist for previous concerts, had presented me with some two-piano music to learn. We would be performing during National Music Week in Corinth in May. It was work, but at the same time it was pure delight, learning and playing the piano numbers with such an outstanding musician as Martha. This would be a one-of-a-kind experience for me, never to be repeated, sadly. The four numbers we performed were:

*Theme from "The Apartment"* by Charles Williams,
        arr. J. Louis Merkur
*Eighteenth Variation from Rhapsody on a Theme of Paganini*
        by Sergei Rachmaninoff
*Scaramouche*
        by Darius Milhaud
*Begin the Beguine*
        by Cole Porter, arr. Cy Walter

A few months later in December, Martha and I would be playing together again, this time the *Messiah,* with Martha on the organ and me on the piano, accompanying the St. Luke UMC choir with Betty Duvall (King) directing. The two-piano music we had performed was well-executed, but the music of the *Messiah* was anointed by the Holy Spirit. That made all the difference, even though the music for both occasions was equally difficult. This was **His** music!

The next school year, 1971-72, was a great success. I continued to be salt and light for Jesus inside and outside the classroom. A group of the Milam Musicmakers visited residents in the nursing home, Belle Vista, and sang for them.

The entire ensemble of Milam Musicmakers left the confines of the school building and

Milam Musicmakers at Belle Vista in Tupelo."

presented a sacred choral concert at my church, St. Luke United Methodist, on March 14, 1972. Our light was shining all over Tupelo, singing the Lord's songs! There were **thirty** of us. When I opened my Bible for a reassuring verse right before we started, I "happened" to turn to I Chronicles 12:18 –

*Then the Holy Spirit came on Amasai,*
*who was chief of the **thirty**, and he said,*

*"We are yours, O David,*
*And with you, O son of Jesse!*
*Peace, peace be to you,*
*And peace be to him who helps you;*
***For your God helps you.***"

That could not have been a coincidence. I felt like God was saying, "Be at peace. I am with you and your girls, all thirty of you, and I will help you." Wow! The concert was beautiful.

Our spring concert in May also went off very well. It would be my last one at Milam. After the program the Milam Music-makers gave me a beautiful sterling silver cross on a long silver chain. Engraved on the cross were the words, "MILAM MUSIC-MAKERS 1971-72." The other chorus classes gave me a beautiful padded book with my name engraved on it, "Your Treasury of Inspiration."[10] This anthology included many prayers and scripture portions among the 1200 selections. From these gifts I got the message that my Christian witness had not gone unnoticed.

Tom Saterfiel, an intern in the principal's office, accompanied some of our songs. Tom also taught my son, Perry, piano lessons at our house, teaching him chords and how to play by ear. Combined with the earlier lessons I had given Perry, plus lessons from Mrs. Ruth Johnston, a local piano teacher, Perry built quite a repertoire of popular songs – "Proud Mary," "Let it Be," and more. Susan also took lessons from me and then from Mrs. Johnston.

Perry and Susan practicing the piano, 1970

In recent years through Facebook I have reconnected with some students from Milam. I discovered that my teaching had been more influential than I thought. Two students, Ruth Bragg (Compton) and Monica Roden (Spencer), have been successful in musical endeavors. Monica said that while she was in my class, she had decided what she wanted to do in life. She was one of the soloists in the spring concert and had an excellent voice. Monica obtained two degrees in Vocal Performance and continues to be a successful director of the North Mississippi Symphony Orchestra Children's Chorus. She teaches private voice and piano lessons, and has managed her family's music store in Tupelo.

---

10  "Your Treasury of Inspiration," compiled by Eleanor L. Doan (Grand Rapids: Zondervan Publishing House, 1970).

Nancy accompanying Milam Musicmakers, 1972

Ruth and I have had good conversations on Facebook, especially about our experiences playing the piano. She said, "I have thought of you so many times and am very thankful for the influence you had in my life. You were in such an awesome position to impact the musical futures of so many, and you did a fabulous job of creating a desire in me to continue participating in choral music throughout my high school and college ... not to mention that you provided my very first music theory training (not sure I appreciated it as much in 7th grade as I would have a little later in life)." In a recent message, Ruth said, "I am loving the opportunities the Lord has given me to serve as pianist for our church as well as accompanist for the kids' program and lead the youth choir. It's been amazing how so much of my early training has come back to "haunt" me. I never wanted to be a choral conductor (and still don't), but I am thankful for the early training I received from you, which then carried on through high school and college." Today Ruth credits me as one of three people who have made a significant musical impact in her life. Wow! That is cause for praising the Lord! I let my light shine for Jesus at Milam Junior High School.

# CHAPTER 16

## CHURCH CHOIR DIRECTOR

My music ministry went in a new direction, seven months after I resigned from Milam. The Lord gave me an assignment as the choir director at St. Luke, beginning in January 1973. I had been singing in the choir since we moved from Corinth in 1967. This was quite a change. I had gone from disciplining students *five days* a week, which took almost standing on my head to get them to learn, to an easy one-hour practice with adults *one night* a week! Wednesday night after the church service was agreed upon as our practice time. After I drove home from each practice and got in the bed, I rehearsed the songs in my head all night long! That was a small price to pay, however, for the joy of directing my Christian friends and singing Christian music exclusively. The choir and I bonded beautifully.

Our third child, James ("Jim") Curtis Petrey, Jr., was born on April 12, 1974. I continued my choir responsibilities. Curtis was now the merchandising and advertising director of the *Tupelo Daily Journal*. Perry was 14, and Susan was 10. It was wonderful having a new baby, but things got more hectic. Instead of slowing down in my choir job, however, I soon began an ambitious project.

In January 1975, I heard the awesome new Gaither musical, *Alleluia! A Praise Gathering for Believers* arranged by Ron Huff, and I was inspired to purchase the books for the St. Luke choir, rehearse it, and **perform it from memory**! When the books came in, I presented my elaborate rehearsal schedule and the goal of a memorized performance. Surprisingly, no one left the choir. Being a small choir, there was a need for outsiders to augment our sound and sing some of the solos. Singers from other churches agreed to participate: Curtis Buskirk, Larry Montgomery, Shirley Dillard, and J.R. and Clara Pegues. We had practice tapes and extra rehearsals. We even had special prayer warriors. We ourselves prayed diligently and rehearsed tirelessly.

After five months of practice, the big night came on June 14, 1975. We had 150 in attendance that Saturday night, a good crowd for St. Luke. We performed *Alleluia!* again the following Sunday night with 250 in attendance. Chairs had to be brought in, filling the aisles! After the first performance a choir member, Reba, admitted I had made a believer out of her. She never thought we could memorize it. Truly, it was miraculous. The Holy Spirit anointed us with such power. Felix Black, a pillar of the church, said it was one of the finest things to happen in St. Luke. The pastor, Crawford Ray, said, "The Holy Spirit was a felt Presence!" The St. Luke choir would present this beautiful musical three more times.

Our fourth child, Bert Williams Petrey, was well on the way at this time and would be born August 24, 1975. I submitted my resignation as choir director at St. Luke United Methodist Church, effective July 1st. I had served as their choir director for two-and-a-half years. My former practice teacher at Milam Junior High School, Shirley Dillard, took the position. With a new baby, a toddler, a teenager, a pre-teen, and my husband, I had my work cut out for me. But I was "brought out of retirement" a few months later, on December 4th, to direct the choir and present the *Alleluia!* once again at St. Luke. That same Sunday we traveled to New Albany First United Methodist Church and presented it at their evening worship service. Years later, I was blessed to hear that a girl was saved that night, hearing the Holy Spirit-anointed music!

# CHAPTER 17

## CALLED TO FULL-TIME MINISTRY

It was on New Year's Day in 1976, that God called Curtis into full-time ministry. Instead of watching Alabama football, his favorite New Year's Day activity, he paid a visit to our former pastor who was now serving a church in Oxford, Mississippi. No sooner had the two of them entered the pastor's office than Rev. Lavelle Woodrick turned around, looked at Curtis, and, like a prophet, said, "You've come to tell me God has called you to preach." Curtis was astounded, and this was just the confirmation he was looking for. It so happened (surely not a coincidence) that Lavelle served on the conference committee for ordained ministry, and he told Curtis the exact steps to take to become a minister in the United Methodist Church! Next, Curtis paid a visit to another former pastor, Bill Appleby, who informed him that an opening for a pastor on the South Pontotoc County charge in Algoma had just come open. He could begin preaching there in a month's time! Again, Curtis was confirmed in answering God's call because appointments are never made in the middle of the year, certainly not in February. Any Methodist knows that appointments are made in June. From then on, Curtis never doubted his call from God.

The Lord had called me on the same day as He called Curtis, so when he returned from talking to Lavelle Woodrick, I was overjoyed with his news. We would have to be moving out of our beautiful spacious home in the country, and we would have to get rid of most of our furniture because the parsonage in Algoma was already furnished. Those facts only heightened my sense of adventure and did not dampen it.

Curtis began the course for his preaching license, which took only a month's time to complete, and then he was officially the associate pastor on a four-church charge. Our new home, Algoma, was smaller than Petrey. The **four** churches were named Algoma, Palestine, Ebenezer, and Fairview. Appropriately, we had **four** children, but we only had **three** bedrooms! Susan was eager to take the utility room and turn it into a bedroom. Problem solved! Another problem – our new salary was only $400 a month. God began to send us money and meet our needs in a variety of ways. Problem solved. We continued to tithe our income like we always had, and the financial miracles abounded. "Life got more exciting with each passing day," as the song says.

Curtis, Nancy, Jim, and Bert at Algoma UMC - Curtis is assistant pastor for four churches, 1976

Being a wife and mother was a time-consuming occupation in those days, but I did participate in the Fairview choir and help with piano playing. We were in Algoma for only one year. Curtis would be attending seminary at the Memphis Theological Seminary. Our next appointment was closer to Memphis – Potts Camp United Methodist Church, a three-point charge. Curtis had been an associate pastor his first year, but now he was the one and only pastor of all these churches, besides commuting to Memphis for seminary and supporting a wife and four children. At least we had a bigger parsonage. I typed Curtis' papers, and I had more opportunities for music ministry.

I played the organ and piano for the Potts Camp church, and I organized a good-sized youth choir. God used me to encourage a man who had a beautiful voice but was scared to sing in public. I told him to take 2 Timothy 1:7 like a medicine, three times a day, saying it out loud – "For God has not given us a spirit of fear, but of power and of love and of a sound mind." He did it, and, gradually, Mitch Stone began to sing more confidently and eventually made recordings. Today, he credits me with advising him and challenging him to rise to his potential.

I encouraged Mitch, and Terri Day (Kitchens), a friend of Susan's, encouraged **me**. Without a cheerleader like Terri in my balcony, I would not have sung many solos.

We served the Potts Camp charge for two years. Then, one day, Curtis got a call from the Bishop. We were about to embark on a different type ministry. It would be like going "from glory to glory!"

# CHAPTER 18

## VACANT LOT AND NO PARSONAGE

One day when Curtis was at the seminary he got a call from Bishop Mack Stokes. Someone in the break room had to find Curtis and get him to the phone, saying with alarm, "The Bishop is on the phone! He has to talk to you!" With no small amount of trepidation, Curtis answered the phone. Bishop Stokes, in his slow Southern drawl, said, "Petrey, my man in Southaven has become discouraged and quit. The cabinet is meeting now, and we all agree you are the man to go up there and make a go of it. What do you think?" After catching his breath, Curtis said, "Well, frankly, Bishop, I'm in shock!"

Curtis told the Bishop he would have to pray about it before giving an answer. Bishop Stokes said they must know in two weeks. When our church members were notified of this, they went into high gear, pulling every string they knew how to pull to keep us at Potts Camp. We dearly loved them, had seen real progress in church growth and were not in a hurry to leave.

Marlon Rains was the pastor we had followed to Potts Camp. He had stayed two years, and we had now served there two years. Then Marlon accepted the challenge to start a new church in Southaven, Mississippi, a suburb of Memphis. This was a unique church in that Marlon was a graduate of Oral Roberts University and had let it be known that Faith United Methodist Church would be a "Spirit-filled" church. When I heard that, my heart leaped! Curtis and I had been filled with the Holy Spirit when we were in Tupelo during the time we met with other church members in a home group. Some people call this the "second blessing." I understand it this way, theologically: When Jesus appeared to His disciples in the upper room after His resurrection, He breathed on them and said, "Receive the Holy Spirit." That is the moment they were born again, regenerated, and the Holy Spirit lived inside them. But on the Day of Pentecost, they were "baptized" in the Holy Spirit, which empowered them to go forth and make disciples.

We had begun traveling in charismatic circles, and our faith had grown by leaps and bounds. The mention of a "Spirit-filled" church fired our expectations of an exciting and fruitful ministry. The other facts about Faith UMC were not so exciting. There were still only twelve members, and there was no church building. They had been meeting in a school. Marlon and his wife, Dinaca, would be selling their house and moving, so there was no parsonage awaiting us! We would have to find our own house. These were sobering facts.

Looking it cold in the face, Curtis was being asked to revive a "stillborn baby" with no parsonage and only a vacant lot! And we had four children to support. The Methodist powers-that-be argued that this was a fast-growing area and needed a Methodist church. The lot was in a strategic place. All that was needed for success was the right minister, and they had decided that Curtis was the man. The District Superintendent, J. W. Chatham, promised to raise the salary and find a house for us. Curtis had two weeks to make a decision, and oh, how we both prayed. Despite the negatives, I was eager for the challenge, and Curtis was, too. A Spirit-filled church!

At the end of two weeks, Bishop Stokes called for the answer. Curtis said, "Well, Bishop, I have really prayed but have not heard God say anything. Since I haven't heard Him say 'No,' then I have to believe that the Lord wants me to accept the appointment to Faith." It was a sad separation from some fantastic people in Potts Camp, but faith was surging in our hearts, and this was apparently our destiny.

We could see God's hand so clearly in our move. We found a house, but it would not be available for two more weeks. The children and I would stay with my parents in Luverne. Paul Baddour, owner of Fred's department stores, offered to load all our belongings on his big truck and keep them until the Southaven house was ready to move into. That was just the beginning of the miracles unfolding in this divine assignment. Since the house had only three bedrooms, Perry would make his bedroom in the small storage building in the back yard. He was quite creative in making it comfortable, the same way Susan had made the utility room in Algoma comfortable.

Right away we visited the church, which at that time was in the middle of a high-profile tent revival meeting on the corner property. The address, interestingly, was 777 State Line Road, and everyone knows that 777 is God's number! It was one street over from the intersection with Airways Boulevard, the street going to the Memphis International Airport. Yes, it was at a strategic location. When we arrived at the tent, Cheryl Prewitt, who would become Miss America 1980 very soon, was sitting at the piano! Another celebrity, operatic star Marguerite Piazza of Memphis, was one of the revival soloists! Our friend, Evangelist Cecil Williamson, was the revival preacher. What a blessing to see our tent revival make headlines on the front page of the Memphis Commercial Appeal. We were being launched in a spiritually spectacular way!

Our move to Southaven was on June 29, 1979, and in October the building started going up. We were in it on New Year's Eve, having our first service by candlelight! The wonders never ceased. We would be at that church for nine years, and during that time there were two more building projects to enlarge the church. The first addition was completed in January 1982, and the new sanctuary (big enough for a gymnasium) was completed in September 1983. The next building project was a beautiful parsonage next to the church. We moved into it in July 1986, and lived there for two years before the Lord moved us again.

My husband Curtis was gifted in preaching. (The first time I heard him preach as a layman a few years before, my mouth dropped open! I was stunned at his gift from God.) Many people came and stayed once they heard him preach. But he was not afraid to share his pulpit, and we were treated to out-

Curtis, pastor of Faith United Methodist Church in
Southaven, MS, March 1981

standing spiritual giants. Being in a suburb of Memphis gave us
unusual opportunities for spiritual food.

Curtis was also gifted in administration. I marveled at the way
he led the board meetings and the respect he commanded from our
members. He got his Masters of Divinity from the seminary, grad-
uating in May 25, 1980. Less than two weeks later at the annual
meeting of the Alabama-West Florida Conference of the UMC, he
was named Top Evangelistic Pastor, and Faith UMC was named the
Top Evangelistic Church, June 1980. It had been just one year since
Curtis became the pastor, and the membership had grown 389 per
cent! The Cecil Williamson Evangelistic Ministry awarded Curtis a
mission trip to the Philippines that year in December. Curtis didn't
know it at the time, but he was paving the way for our son Perry
to also go on mission to the Philippines three years later, acquire a
wife, and eventually give us many wonderful grandchildren! God
always has such good surprises up His sleeve.

# CHAPTER 19

## DEVELOPING THE FAITH FORCE

When we first arrived to pastor Faith UMC, we met at DeSoto County Academy on Goodman Road. Our attendance grew very slowly from the original 12 charter members. A few people expressed an interest in having a choir, so I was glad to meet that need. We started with Gene and Melita Powell (Hood), gathering around the old beat-up piano and singing our hearts out. Our next choir members were Glenn and Pat Roseberry. After we moved into the new building January 20, 1980, and invited people to join, we had twelve members at the first practice. We got a decent piano and sang praise and worship songs, choir anthems, and hymns.

The beauty of the praise and worship songs we sang every Sunday was that they were not just **based** on Scripture, but many of them were direct quotes. I had begun learning Scripture songs back in the late 1960s and 1970s when Curtis and I participated in a home group. To this day I can sing scores of them. What a great way to memorize Bible verses. I sing them around the house and build up my faith. Here are a few favorites:

*1. I can run through a troop and leap over a wall …* (Psalm 18:29)

*2. You are a chosen generation, a royal priesthood, a holy nation, a peculiar people, who should show forth the praises of God, who has called us out of darkness into His marvelous light.* (1 Peter 2:9)

*3. Arise, shine, for thy light has come, and the glory of the Lord is risen upon thee.* (Isaiah 60:1)

*4. It's not by might nor power but by My Spirit, says the Lord …* (Zechariah 4:6)

*5. The law of the Lord is perfect, converting the soul: the testimony of the Lord is sure, making wise the simple. More to be desired are they than gold, yea, than much fine gold: sweeter also than honey and the honeycomb ...* (Psalm 19:7-11)

*6. This is my rest forever, here will I dwell, for the Lord has chosen Zion, He has declared it for His habitation ..."* (Isaiah 132:13-16)

*7. In the presence of Your people, I will praise Your name, for alone You are holy, enthroned on the praises of Israel ...* (Psalm 22:3, 22 and Psalm 145:7)

*8. Thou hast turned my mourning into dancing for me; Thou hast put off my sackcloth ...* (Psalm 30:11)

*9. Beloved, let us love one another, for love is of God, and everyone that loveth is born of God and knoweth God. He that loveth not knoweth not God, for God is love. Beloved, let us love one another, First John four, seven and eight!*

*10. He brought me to His banqueting table, and His banner over me is love ...* (Song of Solomon 2:4)

*11. The Lord thy God in the midst of thee is mighty, is mighty. He will sing, He will rejoice over thee with joy, with joy. He will rest in His love. He will joy over thee with singing ...* (Zephaniah 3:17)

By April, the choir of twelve was ready to present our first musical, *Breakfast in Galilee* by Sonny Salsbury. The choir attempted a difficult musical for Christmas 1980, *His Love Reaching* by Ron Huff and Bill and Gloria Gaither. There were still only twelve of us, but it was gorgeous. Surely angels must have augmented our sound. It was a miracle performance.

I loved to play the piano for the worship services. Over the years we were at Faith, we had several song leaders, and I also led from the piano. At first, we used a little spiral songbook, "Lift Him Up" by Don Marsh. On page 108 was our opening song at every Sunday morning service, "Surely the Presence of the Lord is in This Place." And that was the case because every service we felt the moving of the Holy Spirit. I learned to play all the songs in that book, as well as other songbooks, but still there were so many others I wished we could have in the worship services. It was embarrassing to me that I couldn't even play "Happy Birthday" without the written music!

The ladies of the church planned a special meeting and invited a speaker, Annette Funderburk. After her message she gave a prophecy to me. She said, "You have been wanting to play the piano 'by ear,' and God is about to give you your heart's desire." Her word was true, and it was fulfilled shortly. After that night a church member came to me and made a request for a certain praise song for the congregation to sing. I told her I liked it but couldn't play it because I didn't have the music. She encouraged me to try to play it anyway. To my surprise, I was able to "pick it out" on the piano, and the congregation sang it. This was just the first of many songs I learned to play without the written music. I studied my college textbook of music theory and finally made sense of playing by chords. God had indeed given me my heart's desire!

Later, I began to make piano and voice recordings of praise and worship songs, using the church's sound system and operating it myself. I had to run back and forth from the piano to the sound equipment during the interval between a group of songs or in the case of wrong notes that had to be rerecorded. In our first sanctuary I didn't have to sprint so far. The sound equipment was behind the last pews, but in the new and bigger sanctuary I had to run from the onstage piano through the length of the sanctuary to the sound booth upstairs! Amazingly, the huffing and puffing from my sprints didn't show up on the recordings. I was the recorder and "recordee" over the years and made several cassette tapes full of choice praise and worship music. These tapes were shared for use in private and corporate worship settings. Some of them had both my voice and the piano accompaniment, and some had only the piano music. Recently, our drummer, Steve Rapp, put one of the tapes online. I was surprised at the good quality after all these years.[11] Besides the praise and worship songs, I also recorded music for my solos.

Singing solos was the most thrilling part of my music ministry. When professional solo accompaniments first became available on tapes back in the 1960s and 1970s, I was overjoyed. Singing along with an accompaniment tape was such a glorious experience. A

---

11   Nancy's praise songs - http://bit.ly/PraiseSongs

whole orchestra would back up your amateur skills. And that's what I was, an amateur. I never considered myself a "trained" singer, so I wasn't burdened with a high standard to meet. I simply sang from my heart the wonderful message of the song and reveled in the awesome melodies and harmonies. I felt free as a bird. Playing the piano didn't compare with singing solos for thrills. There was no scarcity of good vocalists in the church, so I had to wait my turn. Usually, I waited for Curtis or someone else to ask me. Curtis loved for me to sing "Standing on Holy Ground" and requested it often.

Singing at the annual Sweetheart Banquets was another opportunity for our members to perform. Directing the choir was hard work, but singing a solo was sheer delight. As Curtis would say, "Get under the spout where the glory pours out!" Yes, there was nothing like the anointing of the Holy Spirit.

Once I had a mono-tone singer in the choir, and I didn't know what to do about it. He loved the Lord, but his voice was so loud. How could I tell him he couldn't sing in the choir? I couldn't. But I did come up with a plan. I announced we were reforming the choir and would have auditions to properly place everyone. Guess what? He didn't come to the auditions. Later, one day in church he said to me, "You didn't have to go to all that trouble of having auditions. I know I can't sing!" Praise the Lord that he was good-natured about it. Unfortunately, attendance at rehearsals began to dwindle. What was the problem?

Nancy singing "My Treasure" at Sweetheart Banquet at Faith UMC, 1987

I was the problem, I had decided. Women should not be directing men. It said so in the Bible. I told Curtis we needed to find a man to replace me as choir director. I resigned. Because of poor attendance at the choir rehearsals, the Council on Ministries agreed that the choir should be discontinued for a month, during which time perhaps a new choir director could be found. The only man who applied for the position had questionable character, and I was in turmoil that he would get the job.

Pat Roseberry spoke at a Wednesday night service and addressed the problem of loss of interest in the choir. She strongly insisted, using Scripture, that the Lord wanted a choir, and there were some people not responding to his call to sing in it. I was more burdened than ever. Louise Earlywine asked everyone to come to the altar and pray. She knelt beside me, prayed for me, and affirmed me as the choir director.

That night I was awakened with this thought – "If your child is bad or if he leaves you, you are still his mother." Then the next thought came – "You are the mother of the choir." Next – "You birthed the choir." My devotional that morning was about a conversation between two pregnant women. One of them said, "Of course there's blood and pain, but there's life at the end." More affirmation came. At a conference in Texas, one of the speakers said that authority was assigned to those who had the training for a particular job, whether the authority was male or female. I knew the Lord was speaking to me, and that He had qualified me for the position I held as choir director, no matter if some of the singers were male. My doubts fled, and my confidence returned.

On Pentecost Sunday, June 7, 1981, the choir of only seven people was reorganized with a new name, the Faith Force, signifying ministers on call, taking music to those in need. We began to minister at the nursing home regularly. Two years later we numbered twenty. In April 1983, the Faith Force presented the same musical the St. Luke choir had performed in 1975, *Alleluia! A Praise Gathering for Believers.* Based on Hebrews 13:15-16, an offering was received during the intermission for the needy in the Philippines.

The Faith Force singing "Alleluia!" by Bill & Gloria Gaither, April 1983

Then we "took it on the road" to Potts Camp UMC and Victoria UMC and at both places received a glowing reception. We were ministers on call, fulfilling our purpose.

It was a great joy to see my singers developing. God had opened my eyes to see the ones who could sing solos, men and women who had never sung a solo in their lives. Despite their protests, I would get them to sing solos and then watch them blossom! I recall one of those was Don Russell, who went into the ministry under Curtis (there were ten in all who answered God's call). Another one was Barbara Butler (Brooks) who had a rich alto voice. I started her off with only one verse of a song. After that debut, she sang solos often. In years to come, after we had left Faith UMC, Barbara became the song leader. It was satisfying to see that I had been a part of the musical growth of my choir members.

My own husband Curtis had always said he couldn't sing, but it was apparent that he loved to sing. When the congregation sang, I could see his mouth moving and a smile on his face. I believe his ability to carry a tune developed the minute he answered the call to full-time ministry. His "pre-call" musical ability was lacking, however. One time I tried to coach him to sing the popular song,

"Some Enchanted Evening." Invariably, he would hit a sour note on the last syllable of "eve-ning" when the melody dipped down low. No matter how much I had him repeat the song, he never could get that note right. Ha! But after the anointing of the Holy Spirit was on Curtis, he sang beautifully.

I was the choir director, song leader, and pianist. I loved it, and it was almost a full-time job. Barbara Butler (Brooks) insisted I get a salary. She lobbied for me at the church board meeting, and I began to receive a little check for my efforts. Hey! I became a "professional" music minister at that point! The Faith Force continued to go outside the walls of the church and bless people in other churches, nursing homes and in prison. On one trip to Parchman Penitentiary, we not only sang but distributed 600 gift packages that had been prepared by the women of the church.

The Faith Force regularly presented Christmas and spring programs each year at our church – *Noel, Jesus is Born* by Lanny Wolfe, Don Marsh, and Bob Benson with 11 members in 1981

The Faith Force Christmas concert, "The Reason for the Season," 1987

and 16 members in 1984, and *The Reason for the Season* by David T. Clydesdale in 1983 and in 1987 with 23 members. That year, 1987, we also presented it at Parchman and at another church.

In 1986 our choir reached its peak with 30 members. This was the largest choir we had in the nine years I was choir director. That Christmas we presented *Sounds of His Love* by Don Marsh and Karen Dean. But the greatest musical accomplishment I had as a choir director was presenting selections from the famed *Messiah* by George Frederic Handel in 1985 in both spring and Christmas concerts. Nothing is more thrilling or full of the Holy Spirit than the "Hallelujah Chorus."

The Faith Force Christmas concert, "Sounds of His Love," 1986

# Chapter 20

## Back to the Classroom

After Jim entered Greenbrook Elementary School, I took a part-time job at Greenbrook Baptist Church right across the street from the school, teaching kindergarten music. Bert was in my class. This was in addition to the music ministry I had at Faith UMC. Can you believe I was terrified to face those little four and five-year-olds? The old fears I had when I first started teaching in 1963 and again in 1968 resurfaced. This was 1980, and I was allowing these little children to scare a 43-year-old woman! I asked my friends to pray for me, and the first day was victorious. My fears were banished, and I had a wonderful time with the children. For their Christmas program I had written a play for them, and it was a great success. For the program at the end of the school year I wrote a special song, "Take Time to Smell the Roses."[12]

> *Take time to smell the roses, Mom, take time to hold my hand.*
> *Take time to hear my problems and to say you understand.*
> *Take time to play a game with me, to throw and catch a ball.*
> *Take time to say you love me and to see I'm growing tall.*
>
> *(Chorus) Take time to smell the roses when they're blooming,*
> *Take time to smell the roses when they're there.*
> *Take time to smell the roses when they're blooming,*
> *For I'm your rose, please show me that you care.*
>
> *Take time to smell the roses, Dad, take time to talk with me.*
> *Take time to let me hug your neck, take time to really see*
> *That I am growing up so fast, I need your help each day*
> *To guide me in the things I do at school and church and play.*
> *(Chorus) — May 1981*

---

12  Appendix: *My Song Compositions*, "Take Time to Smell the Roses," 1

At the end of the song the children took roses to their parents out in the audience. The children and parents loved it.

One of the parents, Bonnie Green, who was also a member at Faith, told me that while I was teaching her children, Dena (Frazier) and Jason, they invited Jesus into their hearts! They were grown by the time I learned of this recently. Bonnie said that they had always looked back to that time as their salvation experience. I know it must have happened when I taught the children the song, "Somebody's Knocking at Your Door." The song had motions, and the door represented the heart. *"Oh, sinner, why don't you answer? Somebody's knocking at your door. Knocks like Jesus ... "* Then we sang the little chorus, *"Into my heart, into my heart, come into my heart, Lord Jesus ... "* I explained to the children about the simple act of faith to open the door of your heart to Jesus, that that was the way to become a Christian. Wow! Even though I taught there a short time, the Lord produced fruit through me.

My next adventure in the classroom was at Horn Lake High School, just down the road from our home in Southaven. The choral music teacher had retired, and the Superintendent called and asked me to take the job, beginning in September 1983. Since Jim and Bert were in school, and Susan and Perry were in college, I accepted. The teacher who had retired was a real pro, and here I was, coming in to carry on the music program with only a few years' experience. This was going to be easier, however, teaching in a high school instead of a junior high, I thought. Besides that, I would have two classes of tenth grade English. That really appealed to me.

The students who signed up for chorus included more boys than I had taught in Montgomery or Tupelo. I can remember two boys who were very helpful to me and were good students, Joe Moore and Jerry Smithey, both strong Christians. I was all set to let my light shine for Jesus. We gave a Christmas concert on the night of the open house. The second semester of the English classes was devoted to literature, so I asked the principal if I could teach Bible along with the other literature. He agreed. Much to my surprise, he directed me to a storage room that was full of Bibles! I was elated!

Nancy at Open House, the night of her
Christmas concert at Horn Lake High School,
MS, 1983

The year concluded with a concert, and the students made me proud. The first year in a new school is always the hardest. Now that I had been "initiated," the second year looked appealing. However, things were getting more exciting and fruitful at Faith. Our second addition to the building had been completed at about the same time I started the job at Horn Lake. The opening service had been on September 11, 1983, and activities at the church were in high gear. Our son, Perry, had gone as a missionary to the Philippines on January 5, 1983, and Curtis and I had been to visit him and his new wife on my school Christmas break. Jim and Bert were more involved in church activities at Faith, and they were at the peak of their soccer careers. My heart was being drawn to church and family more than ever.

Out of necessity many wives can juggle a lot of separate responsibilities. However, I knew that Curtis didn't need a wife with a double allegiance. I could envision my teaching job becoming more important to me than my home, and Curtis and I going in opposite directions with our "careers." I determined I would have to give up my job at Horn Lake. The salary was good, but God had always provided. My teacher's salary could be sacrificed, so I could be a full-time wife, mother, and music minister, not to mention the myriad other tasks required of a pastor's wife.

# Chapter 21

## Growing Family and Ministry

Bert taking piano lessons from his mother, October 1984

Family life and new ministry opportunities grew in intensity in our last five years at Faith UMC. I had always liked variety, so now I had plenty of it. I gave piano lessons to Jim and Bert and others, including adults (some took voice lessons). Jim and Bert, 10 and 11 years old, started listening to Christian contemporary music. I was so proud of them when they sang "Man in the Middle" by Wayne Watson. Their performance, using an accompaniment tape, at church and at a campground, was great. Perry had married a Filipino, Marilou, and adopted her child Franco. Then they had two more children, Joshua and Caleb (P.J.). What fun we had when they came to visit and eventually moved to Horn Lake. Susan graduated from Mississippi State and was married to Russell Zwerg in 1986. That summer we moved into our new parsonage. To say it was a busy time is an understatement.

In October that year Curtis and I attended a Walk to Emmaus weekend in Moscow, Tennessee. It was life-changing, and

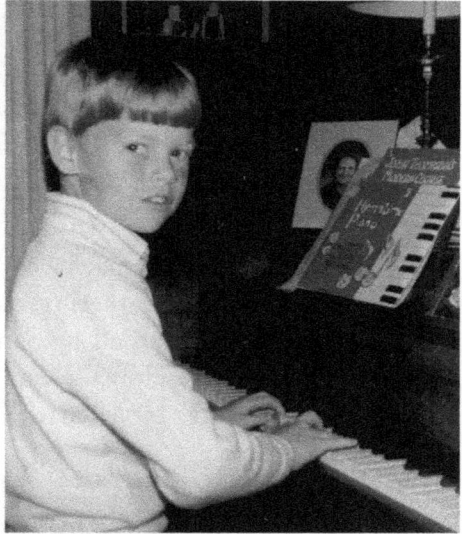

Faith UMC and parsonage, January 1988

we volunteered to serve on Emmaus teams after that. I was blessed to serve in the Prayer Room and sometimes as Music Director, leading the singing from the piano. I learned a whole new repertoire of music. The Emmaus songs were so special. I sang solos during these Emmaus weekends, and I also was asked to sing solos at the reunion gatherings afterward. My song repertoire was growing. Songs recorded by Sandi Patty were my favorites, especially "Standing on Holy Ground" by Geron Davis and "How Majestic is Thy Name" by Michael W. Smith. I had stacks of accompaniment tapes.

Curtis began to serve as Spiritual Director on the Walks, and he was much in demand for many years to come. We got into prison ministry in a big way, and this opened the door for me to sing solos and share my testimony at Parchman Penitentiary, quite a different setting for me.

Curtis and I and others from Faith attended some outstanding conferences. The James Robison Bible Conference in Fort Worth, Texas, in January 1987, was especially impacting. Curtis had gone by himself the year before, and he came home all excited about the music and the song leader, Jeanne Rogers. (Later, we invited her to Faith to lead us in worship.) Curtis was even more excited about James Robison's wife Betty doing an impromptu ballet dance. He wanted to see our church explode in worship like he had experienced in Fort Worth.

A group from Faith attended two more James Robison Bible Conferences, first in Fort Worth and then in Atlanta. It was in the van on the way to Atlanta, May 9, 1987, that I composed a song for our congregation to sing, "It's Time to Move."[13] Not only the Faith Force choir, but the whole congregation was increasingly "moving out" for God! Our music was a catalyst.

I found out how to facilitate this newfound interest in praise and worship by subscribing to Integrity's Hosanna! Music out of Mobile, Alabama. Each month I received a booklet of Songsheets and a cassette tape. I learned every one of the songs and introduced a lot of them into our congregational worship. The choir presented Integrity's medley, "Mighty Warrior," and it was very powerful and a real favorite. My family was used to seeing me in the kitchen, fixing a meal while plugged up to my headset tape player and listening to the Integrity songs.

A drummer named Steve Rapp (perfect name for a drummer!) and his family began attending our church. Steve got permission from the board to use our building for his band rehearsals. He asked Curtis if he could leave his drum set in the room to the side of the stage in the sanctuary. Steve was faithful about storing his drums in that room after each rehearsal, except for one time. One Sunday morning we noticed the drum set was still set up over behind the piano. While I was leading the worship from the piano, Curtis boldly walked out into the congregation and summoned Steve to the drums. That was one of the things I liked most about our worship services. You never knew what would happen next! Steve began to accompany me in whatever style I was playing, whether fast or slow, loud or soft. Immediately, my spirit rose with exhilaration! There was no doubt that Steve was very sensitive to the moving of the Spirit. His drumming never overpowered the music. On the contrary, it definitely enhanced our worship. I loved it. That afternoon the telephone in the home of Debbie Craft, our Chairman of Worship, rang off the hook! The complaints far outnumbered the affirmations of having drums in worship. There was no positive consensus for the drums, it seemed.

---

13  Nancy Petrey, *Habitation of Honey: Poems and Songs* (Gonzalez, FL: Energion Publications, 2015) p. 54.

It just so happened that the next Sunday, February 8, 1987, we were having a guest preacher of great renown, Dr. Michael Brown, the world's foremost Messianic Jewish apologist,[14] for the morning worship service. Dr. Brown had a powerful message that was tailor-made for Faith United Methodist Church. He had fasted and prayed, and the Lord revealed two opposing factions at Faith and how He felt about it. (This paved the way for harmony.) At the end of his message he said, "I noticed you have a drum set over there. I was a rock drummer before I was saved, and every time I go in a church that has drums, I always ask to play them." Oh, what a surprise! A ripple of anxiety was surely coursing through the congregation. Dr. Brown said to me, "Please play the Jewish song you played earlier, and let us sing it again." He positioned himself at the drums, and I played "Celebration Song (In the Presence of Your People)" by Brent Chambers. He tore loose on the drums! We worshiped God in unity, and the air was gloriously cleared.

God had spoken up through Dr. Brown, and the drums were IN! Pretty soon, our musical instruments increased to three with the addition of a guitar, played by Mike Boone.

---

14  Dr. Michael Brown, national and international speaker, adjunct professor in seminaries, author of 27 books, debates Jewish rabbis, agnostic professors, and gay activists, has Ph.D. in Near Eastern Languages and Literatures, founder and president of FIRE School of Ministry in Concord, NC, host of syndicated radio show and apologetics T.V. show – see full bio at https://askdrbrown.org/biography/

# CHAPTER 22

## IN THE GARDENS

Curtis and I became involved in prison ministry through a woman named Barbara Dycus with Second Chance Prison Ministries. We began going down to Parchman Penitentiary with her. They had a new Spiritual Life Center, and programs for the inmates were presented there. Our choir was scheduled to perform in April 1988. Early in the year we began rehearsals for the beautiful musical, *In the Gardens* by Bill and Gloria Gaither, arranged by Mark Hayes.

Prior to this, on October 27, 1987, while listening to a musical program in our church, my left ear began to have a sympathetic vibration with the synthesizer instrument onstage. This reverberation in my left ear increased gradually, until in January my head was filled up with noise! I paid a visit to an ear, nose, and throat doctor. He administered a hearing test and said it showed nerve deafness and a moderate loss of hearing in the low frequencies. He prescribed a decongestant, but he said there was really nothing that could be done about my hearing loss, which he expected to continually get worse! What a shock. Well, if this condition couldn't be fixed medically, then I would concentrate my efforts on seeking God only for my healing. While praying one day, the phone rang, and it was my friend, Louise Earlywine. She had been concerned about me. The Sunday before as I sat on the piano bench and led the singing, I realized I could only hear about 40 per cent of what was going on. I decided right then to turn over all my jobs – pianist, song leader, choir director – to three other people. This was the most traumatic and depressing time in my life. I could not stand to hear the clashing, discordant notes on the piano, distorted by my hearing disability. I stopped playing the piano altogether.

I have a sad memory about this time. When I badly needed comforting, Curtis had gone to play golf (a rare thing for him). It seemed that no one cared. That afternoon only Bert (twelve years old) was home. His hamster had died, and my heart went out to him. He was feeling sorrow, too. With tears, I helped him bury the hamster, and I prayed for God to comfort me, to cause Curtis to feel my pain, and to help me forgive Curtis for not being with me at this critical time.

Louise believed in divine healing also, but she had to tell me about someone she knew who had been helped at the world famous Shea Clinic in Memphis. She urged me very strongly to make an appointment there. I had been standing in faith for God's miraculous touch. Nevertheless, I decided to "put a fleece out." I told Louise, "If I call and find out that the fee is not out of reach and I can get an appointment that day, I will take that as a sign from God that He wants me to go to Shea Clinic." I called, and both conditions were met! It would only cost $90. My appointment would be that day, February 14. Now that was no small miracle.

I drove to Memphis to Shea Clinic. My doctor was Dr. Emmett instead of Dr. Shea. Many tests were administered. Dr. Emmett gave me some good news. Yes, it was nerve deafness, but it was the type that could be treated! He had seen success in these cases. The exact diagnosis was *cochlear hydrops*, a fancy term for "fluid in the inner ears." It was similar to Meniere's Disease, except I had no dizziness. He prescribed aerobic exercise, low-salt diet, and a diuretic. I went to the desk to pay my bill. There was no charge for the visit or the battery of tests! What? This gave me added proof that the Lord had indeed sent me to Shea Clinic. I was informed that Shea Clinic gave free treatment to people in full-time ministry! Oh, what rejoicing went on in the car during my drive back home.

I filled the prescription for steroids to kick-start my treatment. Unfortunately, this medicine increased the roaring in my head to monumental proportions! How would I even go to sleep at night?

Miraculously, I did sleep and slept well. In my "**quiet** time" (even though my head was full of a **loud** ocean) I heard the Lord say, "My grace is sufficient for you." It didn't seem to make sense, but it was true. I felt so cared for by the Lord right in the middle of losing my hearing and the implications of losing my music ministry, which was dear to my heart.

I was zealous in doing my aerobic exercise, but the devil was still alive and well. Surely it was he who gave me a bad cold to add to my already congested head. This was all-out war. I continued anyway, and I also cut down on salt in my diet and took the diuretic medicine. My hearing began to stabilize somewhat. Although the "airplane noise" in my head was still there, I didn't notice it much. At least it wasn't the high piercing sound that most people with tinnitus experience. I was grateful.

One day in March I realized that I needed to call Parchman Penitentiary and tell them our choir would have to cancel the performance of *In the Gardens* set for April. Before I did that, however, I talked to the Lord about it. I asked Him to give me a verse. I had no idea how He might speak to me through a certain verse, but He had done it many times before. I trusted Him, as I opened my Bible at random and put my finger on a verse. Unbelievable! Amazing! In one verse the Lord covered all the bases – choir director, singer, and the Gaither musical! Here it is from Song of Solomon 8:13, and it was dripping with His love. The Beloved (my Savior, Jesus Christ) speaks:

> *"You who dwell **in the gardens**, the **companions** listen for your voice – let Me hear it!"*

It could be no coincidence that the word for "garden" is **plural**! Our musical was entitled the same – *In the **Gardens**.* The gardens referred to in this beautiful resurrection message are Eden, Gethsemane, and the Garden of the Tomb.

The word "companions" must have referred to the **choir.** So what message was the Lord trying to convey to me? The emphasis was on "your voice." God wanted to hear my voice. I concluded that God wanted me to **sing** in the choir, not direct it, and we could still go to Parchman. I began to feel joy and confidence, so I went to the piano and started to play. It had been so long since I had played. The song that came to mind was an old one from my mother's era, "Indian Love Call." Ooh! It sounded so pretty, and the notes were no longer discordant. Yes, my hearing had greatly improved.

About that time the telephone rang. It was the man who had taken over the choir from me, Dean Murrah. Before I had time to ask the question about his taking the choir to Parchman to sing *In the Gardens,* he began a litany of woes. Dean said, "My wife is getting tired of our Sunday night choir rehearsals cutting in on our family time. She is threatening to divorce me if I don't quit. When are you coming back?" I had not been expecting this, but even as I talked to him, I began to realize how the Lord had already answered Dean's question. The words to *"Indian Love Call"* are "When I'm **calling** you-oo-oo-oo-oo, will you answer too-oo-oo-oo-oo." The Lord was **calling** me back to direct the choir! Dean was waiting for the answer. It was obvious now. I quickly reassured Dean that he must not think of leaving the choir. We badly needed his beautiful tenor voice. Then I said, "I'm coming back!"

My daughter Susan was in the choir, so I told her she would have to help me stay with the beat when rehearsing *In the Gardens* because I couldn't hear the accompaniment tape perfectly. Nevertheless, the rehearsals went well, and we kept our engagement at Parchman. It was customary for an invitation for salvation to be given after each program. Curtis, our pastor, was the obvious one to issue the invitation to the inmates, which he had done many times before. Unfortunately, he said he could not go with us. I reluctantly accepted the task and got several people to pray for me to be led of the Holy Spirit. This was a key moment because eternal outcomes would be decided for those men.

The musical was a resounding success. The final number was "I've Just Seen Jesus," the words of Mary Magdalene to the disciples after she had seen and talked with the risen Christ. When the last note was sung, I turned around to face a packed house of prison inmates. I said, "The first person to tell the good news that Jesus had risen from the dead was a **woman**, Mary Magdalene. And **I** am a **woman**. I am telling you some good news and giving you the opportunity to be forgiven of all your sins and receive eternal life because of Jesus' sacrifice for you. Who will take me up on this offer?" One man came forward to the altar, then two more, and then thirty-nine in all! I led them in prayer to receive Jesus Christ as their personal Lord and Savior. Wow! What a victory for the choir and for me to present this awesome message in music and be instrumental in 39 men being gloriously saved. My light was shining brightly for Jesus, even though I was a hearing-impaired choir director!

# CHAPTER 23

## SONGS THAT MADE A DIFFERENCE

I have vivid memories of several occasions in my life when the Lord spoke to me through a song. These five songs from 1978 to 1988 are examples. The first one is "You Needed Me" by Randy Goodrum.[15] One day our daughter Susan, who was 14 at the time, called me into her room at the parsonage in Potts Camp, Mississippi. She wanted me to hear the music on her radio and said, "Listen to this song. You will love it." She was right. It immediately touched my heart. *"I cried a tear, you wiped it dry, I was confused, you cleared my mind ... somehow you needed me. ... You held my hand when it was cold. When I was lost you took me home ... You even called me friend ... "* Although it wasn't a "Christian" song per se, I interpreted it that way. Through the words I felt like God was saying to me that He needed me, He was someone who cared, and He even called me "friend." This gripped me, to think that **God actually needed me**.

Sometime after that I was driving our three-year-old son Bert and his friend Holly to Wall Doxey State Park not far away. It was a good place for them to romp and play in the leaves and on the play equipment. They were in the back seat. As we rode along I decided to turn on the radio, thinking of how nice it would be to hear "You Needed Me." I was shocked - it was playing! At the precise moment when Anne Murray was singing the words, "**You held my hand** when it was cold," Bert reached over from the back seat and **grabbed my hand**. The presence of God filled the car! That

---

15  Randy Goodrum, "You Needed Me," was the number one hit single in the U.S. in 1978 for Canadian singer, Anne Murray.

was no coincidence. Yes, God was saying that He needs **me**, but I knew more than ever that I need **Him**. He is **everything** I need.

A few years later I heard the song, "The Rose" by Amanda McBroom.[16] It also was not a "Christian" song, but I was very deeply moved to tears when I heard it and knew it must have been inspired by the greatest songwriter of all, the Holy Spirit. I read a newspaper article about how the song was written, which convinced me it was given by God. I cried every time I heard it. McBroom said she was driving down the road while listening to a song on the radio. She didn't agree with the song lyrics about love and began to ponder about what love was to her. She said, "Suddenly, it was as if someone had opened a window in the top of my head. Words came pouring in. I had to keep reciting them to myself as I drove faster and faster towards home … I screeched into my driveway, ran into the house … and sat down at the piano. Ten minutes later, THE ROSE was there."[17]

*Some say love, it is a river that drowns the tender reed.*
*Some say love, it is a razor that leaves your soul to bleed.*
*Some say love, it is a hunger, an endless aching need.*
***I say love, it is a flower and <u>you</u>, its only seed.***

....

*When the night has been too lonely and the road*
*has been too long,*
*And you think that love is only for the lucky*
*and the strong,*
***Just remember in the winter far beneath***
***the bitter snow***
***Lies the seed that with the <u>sun</u>'s love in the spring***
***becomes The Rose.***

---

16  Amanda McBroom's "The Rose," was made famous by Bette Midler who recorded it for the soundtrack of the 1979 film, *The Rose*, in which it plays under the closing credits. It hit number one all over the world in 1979.
17  https://amcbroom.com/about/the-rose/

The message was that love was worth waiting for, worth the hurts and disappointments in the search for it. To me, the rose represented the Seed who was planted in the soil of my barren heart on the day I invited Jesus in to be my Lord and Savior. In the lyrics I also saw Jesus as the sunshine (Son's love) that made the Seed burst into full bloom (God's love) in my heart. The closing lines are a picture of the Resurrection as well as a picture of our salvation, our regeneration by the Seed of the Word planted in us. So beautiful! A song of hope.

How could a secular song have such a deep effect on me? God was teaching me that He could use worldly people to do His bidding. Amanda McBroom thanked everyone who helped her to get the song out to the public, saying she was "eternally grateful" for them, "… and to the Universe for speaking to me in the first place and for showing me what I truly believe." I knew that what Amanda called "the Universe" was really the Holy Spirit.

Another song God used to speak to me was "I Can See" by David Meece and Gloria Gaither.[18] This was a Christian song, and the words are a description of two disciples meeting Jesus on the road to Emmaus (Luke 24: 13-35). Here is an excerpt:

*All at once He walked beside me like He'd been there*
*all along.*
*Not a stranger but a Father who can sense*
*when something's wrong.*
*And He answered all my questions and He understood*
*my fears*
*That somehow vanished now that He was here. (Chorus)*
*I couldn't bear for Him to leave me, so I begged Him*
*please to stay,*
*Spend the evening, a few moments before He went*
*His way.*
*Then like a host He stood and blessed me, broke the bread*
*and poured the wine.*

---

18   "I Can See" by Gloria Gaither and David Meece, Meese Music, 1985

*Then I knew there was something there I recognized.*

*(Chorus) Yes, I can see who walks with me, I can hear who speaks my name,*
*I can feel something stirring in my heart, how His words ring strong and true*
*Like a once familiar strain, and I know I'll never be the same. ... I can see.*

I got a call from a lady, inviting me to sing at the upcoming Walk to Emmaus gathering in Memphis. I immediately knew I must sing "I Can See," because no song could fit the occasion better. Curtis and I arrived early, and we went to the auditorium to set up my tape player. I was surprised to see someone practicing a song with her piano player. To my chagrin I learned that she was going to sing at the gathering! Did that mean that I wouldn't be singing after all? There were two parts to the meeting, first a gathering of the larger Emmaus community, then a prayer service for the new pilgrims on the current Walk. I got it confirmed that I was supposed to sing at the prayer service. My song was very dramatic, and a quiet song would fit in better, I thought. I had brought a second accompaniment tape just in case, "Sweet Hour of Prayer." It would be a great disappointment, however, if I couldn't sing the song that was so perfect for Emmaus, "I Can See." The meeting had begun, and I still couldn't decide between the two songs. *What should I do?* I asked the Lord. I opened the pew Bible and looked down to see if the Lord would point out a verse to me. What a shock! I had turned to the passage about the two disciples on the road to Emmaus! It wasn't the familiar Luke passage, but the two-verse account in Mark 16:12 – "After that, He appeared in another form to two of them as they walked and went into the country." I could hardly take it in that God had spoken to me so clearly. I didn't even know the story was in Mark. Confidence filled my heart, and I sang the divinely appointed song, "I Can See." Yes, it was pretty loud for a prayer service, but I didn't worry. Then there was so much time left that I sang "Sweet Hour of Prayer." As soon as the service was over, some of the Emmaus leaders hurriedly approached me about being the music leader for the next Walk to Emmaus. Evidently, the Holy Spirit had touched them because I let my light shine!

"Take Time to Smell the Roses" was my own composition, but God used it to speak to **me**. I can remember the scene in Columbus at the Central UMC parsonage. I was in the kitchen, working away and singing my song (probably practicing for Mother's Day): *Take time to smell the roses, Mom, take time to hold my hand. Take time to hear my problems and to say you understand. Take time to play a game with me,* ***to throw and catch a ball ....***" And **at that very moment** my teenage son Bert called me from the backyard to come out and **throw the ball to him!** I got the message loud and clear, and I determined to pay more attention to my children.

"All Things" by Chris Christensen was a song taken from Scripture which was recorded by Don Moen. It is based on Romans 8:28 – "All things work together for the good of those who love you ... When things are beyond my control, to You, Lord, I lift up my soul; and when things are hard to understand, Lord, I trust in Your perfect plan ..." This song was playing on the radio, and I was singing along as I looked at the mail. There was an interesting brochure, "Kids with Character." I read:

> Kids with Character is an organization devoted to providing positive role models and positive experiences for the youth of Columbus and Lowndes County. The organization has a simple message that it wants to convey to the youth of today: stay in school, stay away from drugs, and stay out of gangs. Kids with Character was formed in October 1988 after *a local youth was robbed and stabbed while walking home from a high school football game*. That event, along with rumors of gang problems growing in Columbus, spurred eleven residents of the county to action. The group decided to form Kids with Character in an effort to do something about the problems facing today's young people.

**That "local youth" was our son Jim!** On September 30, 1988, Jim had attended a high school football game at the stadium downtown and was walking home. Two teenagers came up behind him. One demanded money, and when Jim didn't have any, the boy stabbed him in the back and then cut him on the neck! Jim saw a policeman across the street and ran to him. The boys scattered. The policeman called for an ambulance to take Jim to the hospital. Then he called us, and we hurried to the hospital. What horrible news to find out that our son had been stabbed! While waiting to see Jim, I held hands with Curtis, our friend Esther, and a chaplain, and we prayed. I prayed that Jim would recover quickly, that he wouldn't have any hate in his heart, and that his attacker would be caught right away and be saved. Curtis and I went back to see Jim.

The doctor told us that Jim's lung was slightly deflated, but that it would spring back in a few days. What a relief! I thanked the Lord that not only would Jim be fine physically but that he had forgiven his attacker. Oh, God's amazing grace! This happened on Friday night. Jim was back in school on Tuesday! He couldn't play soccer for a few weeks. In just two weeks, Jim's attacker, Stephen Jennings, was arrested. He pled guilty and was sentenced to ten years in prison.

Curtis and I had joined Lowndes County Prison Fellowship, a ministry led by Ken and Joyce Linton, and we were going down to Parchman Penitentiary monthly. In July 1990, our group was having a service at Unit 29. I led the singing. Joyce Linton gave a message on forgiveness. Another woman spoke, and she pointed out that it was not God's will for these inmates to wind up in prison. However, since they did wind up in prison, they were not in that room by accident but by divine appointment. How true that proved to be. My husband gave the invitation, and six men came forward. Curtis prayed with them individually to receive Christ.

When we looked at the follow-up cards these six men had filled out, we saw the name of the man who had stabbed Jim! He didn't know us, and we didn't know him. As he was leaving the room, we ran to him and assured him that we had forgiven him and had been praying for him. It was obvious that God had orchestrated the whole thing. What a miracle! We praised God for answering our prayers!

But that's not the end of the story. Stephen Jennings and I wrote letters back and forth. In August 1992, he attended a Kairos weekend at Parchman (like a Walk to Emmaus) and was one of a group of 42 inmates who experienced God's love in an overwhelming way. I was at the closing service, but he didn't know I was there. Stephen was the first one to get to the microphone and testify to an audience of several hundred people how God's love had touched him. Later, we received a letter from Stephen's table leader, giving us details about his participation in his small group. He had introduced himself and said he was at Kairos III because Nancy Petrey had recommended it to him. He took a leadership role at his table and impressed the ministers. Oh, what a blessing to see how God was making a triumph out of a tragedy! About this time Jim was going to YWAM (Youth With a Mission) to their Discipleship Training School in Tyler, Texas, and was preparing for a mission to Romania. God "is able to do exceedingly abundantly above all that we ask or think" (Ephesians 3:20). Wow!

After Jim was stabbed four years earlier, a member of our church, Steve Ellis, wanted to do something to help kids stay out of

James Curtis (Jim) Petrey, Jr., 1992

gangs and off drugs and stay in school. Kids with Character was the result. Professional football players were brought in for a two-week summer camp with boys, teens and younger, at no cost. It was very successful and expanded to other sports and began to include girls. President Bush recognized Kids with Character as one of the Points of Light, and Steve Ellis got to ride in the President's motorcade in Birmingham, spending two hours with him!

Just to think that Curtis was the one to lead Jim's attacker to the Lord! Jim was healed, and I saw all my prayers answered! Isn't it fantastic how *"**All things** work together for the good of those who love the Lord and are called according to His purposes"*? The song, "All Things," was playing, when I first saw the Kids with Character brochure!

What a difference these five songs made in my life. Through them, and through many more songs, God spoke to me and touched me. Jesus is such a wonderful and **personal** Savior!

# CHAPTER 24

## BACK TO A TRADITIONAL CHURCH

In 1988, when Curtis told me we were leaving Faith and moving to Columbus, I was devastated! I was sure that Curtis had not heard correctly from the Lord. Then the Lord sent four members of the church to visit me, one at the time. I knew it really was God who had sent them because He used their words of comfort to help me accept the move. It had been a wonderful nine years at Faith UMC in Southaven. My music ministry was in full bloom, and I could see the fruit of it. Susan and Russell, who were both in the choir, would soon be moving to San Antonio. Perry had served as the children's and youth director, but he and his family of five were planning to move back to the Philippines. We had wise elders. A good pastor, Doug Hardin, a friend of ours, had been appointed to follow us. The Faith folks were the hardest-working, faith-filled people I had known, and I loved them dearly, but God was leading us south. The church would be in good hands. The going-away party for us was awesome.

Curtis Petrey family leaving Faith UMC, June 1988

We needed to be closer to our aging parents in south Alabama. In June 1988, Curtis was appointed to Central United Methodist Church in Columbus, Mississippi, right across the street from Mississippi University for Women. The building was beautiful. This was a traditional Methodist Church, different from the Spirit-filled church we had served for nine years, but it was easy to love the people, and I got involved right away. These were people of faith, too, but they were more reserved in their expression of worship. Jim and Bert were young teenagers. Because gang activity had increased in Columbus, I made the decision to homeschool them, starting with Bert and then with Jim, a year and a half for Bert and a year for Jim.

I joined the Central adult choir and really enjoyed it under Sue Burkhalter's direction. One night at choir practice, John East, an excellent tenor, was making everybody laugh. It was late when I got home and retired for the night. The next morning, I woke up, thinking about John, and began to laugh all over again! Very quickly, a song came to my mind, based on Proverbs 17:22 – *"A merry heart doeth good like a medicine."* The words flowed into my mind from various Psalms. I wrote the words and chords down. Then I figured out a piano accompaniment with runs that mimicked laughter. It was so much fun, singing and playing it. My friend, Esther Troskey, asked me to sing it over and over. "A Merry Heart"[19] was the third song I had composed. It felt good to laugh and to sing the happy words of Scripture. I was sure the Lord had given it to me.

Jim and Bert were in the Central youth group, so I decided to form a Youth Choir. After we invested a lot of work in learning our music, I determined we should not only sing our specials in church, but we should go outside the walls of the church and take a blessing where it was needed most. I got us an engagement at Parchman Penitentiary. A few parents were uneasy about their teenage children being exposed to "prisoners," and one parent would not let her daughter attend. Nevertheless, we took our music "on the road," November 13, 1988, and presented the Integrity Hosanna! Music medley, "Mighty Warrior," at the Spiritual Life Center. We had worked really hard and memorized the whole thing! The inmates

19  Appendix: *My Song Compositions*, "A Merry Heart," 2

Youth Choir of Central UMC, Columbus, MS, singing at Parchman Penitentiary, November 1988

gave us a warm reception. At first some of the youth were afraid, but they finally relaxed and realized they were safe. A few months later in May 1989, we went back again. There were fewer youth, but they did a great job, singing "Forever Grateful," another Integrity Hosanna! Music medley, which we memorized. The following Christmas the Youth Choir presented *Christmas Lights* to the church on December 10, 1989. Recently, one of the youth, Lezli Burt told me, "You worked hard with us. I will never forget you getting

Nancy and Youth Choir leading inmates in singing

put out with our teenage antics and silliness, and you finally had enough and yelled, 'STOP ALL THIS NONSENSE AND SING FOR JESUS!'"

I didn't have nearly as many responsibilities at Central as I did at Faith, but in the area of music during the three years we were at Central I had opportunities to let my light shine for Jesus, speaking and singing in a variety of places. Right after we moved I began attending monthly meetings of the Christian Women's Fellowship, an interdenominational group of Spirit-filled ladies. I was asked to give my testimony at their December 1988, meeting. I was really worried about it because all the speakers I had heard gave very dramatic testimonies, and my testimony was nothing to compare with theirs, I thought. What would I say? One morning I woke up with a song in my heart. The words of the song gave the Lord's answer. *"Share His love by telling what the Lord has done for you."*[20] With renewed confidence, I did just that. My testimony was interspersed with seven songs. Afterward, many people came up for ministry. As I spoke encouraging words to them, prayed for them, and laid my hands on them, I was astounded at the results! Several were "slain in the Spirit!"[21] (John 18:3-6) I left that meeting floating on air and marveling that God had used me in such a supernatural way!

The attendance at the worship services at Central had greatly increased since Curtis became the pastor. I was asked to direct an Easter drama and to write the script. It took place outside and inside the building. We even had a donkey for Jesus' triumphal entry into Jerusalem on Palm Sunday. Unfortunately, the donkey balked, and Jesus had to walk, not ride!

This drama drew a lot of people from all over Columbus. It was a "traveling" audience, since the scenes changed locations, from rooms inside the building, then to the outside, to the courtyard,

---

20   "Share His Love" by William Jensen Reynolds, ©1973.

21   Sociologist Margaret Poloma has defined slaying in the Spirit as "the power of the Holy Spirit so filling a person with a heightened inner awareness that the body's energy fades away and the person collapses to the floor."

to an upper room inside, to the sanctuary, and, finally, ending in the basement with the resurrection scene. What an experience. The Lord was teaching me to do drama as well as music.

The Easter drama didn't include music. However, in Central's worship services I often sang solos and was well received. My hearing loss had stabilized. The hearing tests at Mississippi University for Women Speech and Hearing Center still showed a loss of hearing in both ears in the lower frequencies, especially the left ear, but I could function fairly well, musically. Conversation in groups was the hardest for me. I continued to exercise, but I wasn't as faithful to a low-salt diet as I should have been. The diuretic sapped my energy, so I called Dr. Emmett to ask him if I could discontinue taking the diuretic and just depend on God for His divine healing. Dr. Emmett believed in divine healing also, and he heartily agreed!

The third year we were at Central, Curtis started an early morning service, so that Christian friends from other churches could attend and hear his preaching on the gifts of the Spirit. Through our prison ministry and Curtis' work as president for the local Habitat for Humanity ministry, we got to know people from all over the city besides our church members, and we formed bonds of friendship. At these early morning services at Central, I provided the music, playing the piano and leading the singing, along with singers, a violinist and a guitarist from other churches. It was at this early service that John East and I sang the duet, "I've Just Seen Jesus" by Bill and Gloria Gaither, for Easter 1990.

Our son Perry came from the Philippines to visit us the summer of 1990. I flew back to the Philippines with him for a three week visit and to assist him in a little mission work, August 16th to September 6th. Besides playing with my four grandchildren – Franco, Joshua, Caleb, and Anna – I helped Perry and Marilou give out food and supplies to the poor people around Dumaguete City. On one of these occasions I gave a message and Marilou interpreted for me. I was so scared.

*It is an honor to be here with you. I come in the name of*
*Jesus. How many believe in Jesus Christ? (Hands raised.) "For*

*God so loved the world ..." (John 3:16-17). God so loved **you**
that he **gave** ... his **best** .... It is more blessed to give than receive
.... Go and share with your friends and neighbors. "Give, and it
shall be given to you ...." I have given this from Christian friends
in America in the name of Jesus, not my name. I am blessed to be
able to give this. I want to be your friend. Have a good day.*

I said a lot more, including about the Holy Spirit living in us.
Perry said it was good, that I could preach! I gave the glory to God.
Many thanked me.

I had another opportunity to minister. Pastor Cuasito, the
man who had hosted Curtis on his first mission to the Philippines,
as well as Perry, since he arrived in January 1983, asked me to
sing and testify at his church. I was happy to accept. I told about
God's restoring my hearing enough to lead the Faith UMC choir at
Parchman when 39 men were saved. I also told about our son Jim's
stabbing and his attacker being led to the Lord in prison by Curtis.
Then I sang "He's Ever Interceding" and "Broken and Spilled Out."
I was warmly received, and Cuasito asked me to sing again at the
evening service.

As it turned out, I couldn't go. It seemed that I might be
catching the cold that Perry had been battling. I felt that I needed
to stay home, rest and heal. It was only two days before I would
be flying out of Manila. Cuasito said that I was really anointed,
and the people wanted copies of my tapes. He and his wife came
to visit the next day, and I gave him the tapes. He said that many
came to the church the night before, expecting to hear me sing!
What a blessing that the Lord allowed me to let my light shine for
Him in the Philippines.

That same August 1990, the Lord gave Curtis a vision of Jesus
in an open field outside Columbus with His hands outstretched,
saying, "Come unto me all you that labor and are heavy-laden,
and I will give you rest." Later, the words, "Build it, and they will
come!" came to Curtis and lodged in his spirit. Yes, that was a line
from the movie, *Field of Dreams,* a story with new-age overtones.
However, this concept of acting in faith and seeing Jesus do mira-

cles was valid. Besides, there were quite a few people in Columbus who had the same vision and were just waiting for the Lord to send a man to implement it. Our time at Central was drawing to a close.

# CHAPTER 25

## A GOLDEN TRIANGLE CHURCH

The "field of dreams" turned out to be ten acres of land in a strategic location in Lowndes County, Mississippi, between Columbus, Starkville, and West Point. It was near the exit for the Golden Triangle Airport. Curtis and I first revealed the vision to Dr. Charles and Martha Stanback and Tommy and Julia Ann Glenn. The Stanbacks had a background in Emmaus, like we did, and Martha had a monthly in-home praise, prayer, and Bible study group, which I and Julia Ann had been attending. Martha was also the president of the Women's Christian Fellowship in the city. These couples, along with many others, were so glad to hear of Curtis' vision.

On February 16, 1991, 28 people gathered at the Stanbacks' house to form **Golden Triangle Trinity Church**. There could be no more appropriate name than "**Trinity**," because our location was very near the Golden **Triangle** Airport. A triangle has **three** equal sides, just as the Godhead has **tri-unity**! The **Golden** triangle of our church was Father, Son, and Holy Spirit!

The meeting started with praise – I led in singing, and Martha played the Omnichord (an electronic autoharp). Here I was back in the type of music ministry I had at Faith UMC. The minutes of the meeting that my friend Esther took are such a blessing to read. She recorded every detail of Curtis' vision, which was nothing short of "church utopia!" He started with his testimony of attending the Christian Women's Fellowship that morning in a state of frustration because of a flat tire. He had hurriedly grabbed a Bible at the last minute, not the one he normally used. Esther wrote, "When he got to CWF he opened his Bible & there was a paper in the form of a fish. As he read what was on this fish, he almost disrupted the meeting. It seems that on January 1, 1990, at the intercessory prayer meeting the Lord had told him to cut some fishes out and have each person write the greatest desire of their heart, to put this in their Bible for safe keeping and to remind them of what they were asking from the Lord. His fish had written on it that he wanted to pastor a Spirit-filled church!"

Curtis' vision was for the morning worship service of the new church to be "a ministering and outreach service, with praise and worship, openly charismatic.... Curtis won't do the ministry—WE WILL. ... Lunch will be provided afterward by a Lunch Bunch ministry, mainly for new folks." The evening service would be a family-type service with body ministry, to recognize and know the gifts of the Spirit and learn how to minister. There would be sharing and no "sermon-soaked saints!" We would join with ministries like Crisis Pregnancy Center, Prison Fellowship, and Habitat for Humanity. Curtis wanted to see balance in the body. He expected us to "out-praise the Pentecostals, out-mission the Methodists, and out-baptize the Baptists!"

Curtis said we could share the vision and dream with others but to leave him out of it until March 1st. He would have to tell Central UMC, and he didn't want the news of a new church to leak out. Curtis' appointment would end in June, but he didn't know if the hierarchy would give him "the right foot of fellowship" in March! Curtis also presented his ideas for the government of the church and for an Academy of Faith (various courses) at the Sunday school hour. He said we would have in-home meetings (community groups) in the three-city area and not have meetings at the church on Wednesday nights. So much more was presented in the vision. Curtis emphasized that this church would not be a "Holy Ghost Bless-Me Club," or it would die.

It was decided that the men would meet a few days later at Ken Linton's house. Committees were formed, and it was decided to rent a parsonage. The people who were joining us in Curtis' vision were the cream-of-the-crop. This rented house was soon transformed by volunteer labor and gifts of furnishings and decorations. Some of the ladies who sewed slipcovers for a sofa were not even joining Trinity, but they fully supported us. The Lord had given us favor everywhere we turned. Our family went on a short vacation, and the volunteers insisted we not return until the house was completely finished. We moved in March 22, 1991.

As soon as Curtis informed Central UMC of our plans, the Bishop and cabinet decided to terminate the appointment in March and not wait until June. It was a smooth transition, and the members of Central showed us great love and appreciation with a $500 gift. On our last Sunday, March 3, the District Superintendent was in charge of the morning worship service. He called Curtis to the pulpit and called me out of the choir to stand beside him. The D.S. said, "I have never been more proud of Curtis and Nancy Petrey. Curtis is leaving a secure income and other benefits in the Methodist Church. He reminds me of a man named Abraham, whom God called to leave Ur of the Chaldees." Later the D.S. came by the house to pick up Curtis' credentials, and he said to me, "I am so thankful that Curtis did not split the church. His leaving was peaceful." Actually, there were only two members that left with us, Wanda Burkhalter and Esther Troskey. However, some more families left later.

It was so obvious that the Lord was calling us and providing for us in this step of faith to form a brand new interdenominational church. Our hearts were overflowing with gratitude. What awesome music ministry awaited me. My excitement level was off the charts!

Our first meeting of Trinity Church was at the Regency Park Inn on March 17, 1991, with 80 people attending. The manager, Faye Martin, gave the room to us rent-free for six weeks, and she joined us. Then we rented the old Cumberland Presbyterian Church building in downtown Columbus. Our attendance exceeded 100. We had 62 charter members. At the end of 1991, we had 78 members and 39 families. We were growing fast. Ten acres of land were purchased on Highway 82 West, architectural plans were drawn up, and we would be breaking ground on September 5, 1993.

A couple named Allan and Paula Randle lived next to our plot of ground. Paula was a faithful church member of Evangel Assembly of God, but Allan would not attend church. Paula used all her powers of persuasion on Allan to attend church with her, but he continually refused. One day she angrily said, "When are you ever going to go to church with me?" Allan quickly retorted, "The day they build a church right there in that field!" He pointed to our land! Later, when he saw our church building going up, he knew his unchurched days were numbered. Not long after Trinity Church had the dedication service, Allan and Paula began to attend. Soon they joined, and Allan became a "fanatic for the Lord." He eventually led a group in their home. This was even more confirmation that the Lord had raised up Trinity Church in the Golden Triangle.

Outreach was the very heart of Trinity Church, both within the walls during worship services, then within the city, and, finally, into foreign countries. At the end of 1992, Curtis reported that Trinity supported 18 different missions. The missionaries we supported came to the church to report on their mission results. This inspired some of our members to go on foreign mission trips. Curtis and others went to Romania several times. Two members went to Russia. A family, Will and Eve Lewis and their children, went to Scotland. One member went on YWAM's Mercy Ship to do medical missions. Curtis and I took some members to Israel on missions. It truly was remarkable how God used those who were willing to "go and tell." But there was a mission field close to our church, a black community. Black children would often come into the building out of curiosity. I became church secretary shortly after we moved in the church building downtown. The children would come in the office, and I would get into conversations with them and find out their family situations. Some had parents in prison. They were rough kids but very cute, I thought.

Curtis had a vision for a Vacation Bible School in the black community. Pastor Johnnie Bradford of Open Door Full Gospel

Children's Ministry approached Curtis for help. Our church organized "Kids Count Day Camp" in their building on August 3-5, 1992. Each day ended with lunch. It was a full program. Thirty of our members hosted it, and we had 70 children. I was in charge of the music. It was great fun, teaching praise choruses to the children, especially the songs with hand motions. At the end of the camp 26 children were saved!

We went back the next summer at an open-air location in the middle of a housing project. We had a full praise team on a stage (truck trailer) and all kinds of activities. Some of the kids began coming to our Sunday night children's program. I took a group, named them "Black Diamonds," and taught them some songs, which we presented in a Sunday night worship service, October 1993. The third year for the Kids Count program was on Clover Street. Denise Collins and I led the music under a tent.

Trinity Church directing Kids Count in housing project in Columbus, MS, July 1994

The Trinity children's ministry was going great guns! After we moved in our new building, we needed a bus ministry so we could "import" the children. Jim Collins, a former Lieutenant Colonel in the Air Force, formed a Royal Rangers organization[22] for the

---

22  A mentoring program for future men to form Christ-like character. http://royalrangers.com/aboutus/mission/

boys. It was very successful for our own children and also for the ones brought in by bus.

Our first service in the new building was on August 14, 1994. By December we had to add a temporary building to house the growing children's ministry. Two years later we only owed $190,000 on a $750,000 facility. What a miracle! In March 1997, plans were underway to build a new education building. People were hungry spiritually. They were being fed and given opportunity to minister themselves, and their gratitude showed up in generous offerings.

One of Trinity's biggest outreaches was presenting the drama, *Heaven's Gates & Hell's Flames* in January 1995. Our members formed the cast. I was the "old woman." We had overflow crowds for four nights, and 250 people received Jesus as Savior and Lord! What a privilege it was to be one of the counselors. Pictures of the drama were on the front page of the Columbus Dispatch. We presented this drama again the next year. There was an ice storm, but the weather improved enough to go on with the show, and 96 people made decisions for Christ! God had told Curtis, "Build it, and they will come." We built it, and they did come. It was a beautiful sight to see the headlights of a long line of cars and buses, with people inside them waiting to experience the awesome moving of God in that drama.

# CHAPTER 26

## LEADING THE PRAISE TEAM

The music ministry was always a drawing factor for Trinity. When we started in 1991, I was back to leading the worship from the piano, like I did at Faith UMC, but now I would be leading a team with more instruments. Mark Young, a trumpet player, joined us. His wife Sydney had a solo voice. Our drummer was Jeff Smith. Mary Lou Lake played guitar and piano and sometimes led worship. Bob Boisseau from First Baptist of Columbus joined us with his guitar. Bob was good, but he had no experience on a praise team. Today he will say, "Nancy taught me everything I know." He developed very fast, and in years to come he would be in charge of the praise and worship at other meetings, along with his wife Pat who became an ordained preacher. Other singers were Inez Townsend, Chris Hayes, Karen Cooley, and Randy and Debbie Hays. Randy had led worship in a previous church, so he was put in charge of the evening worship service. Later, Mary Ann Fugitt and Margaret Ann Chandler joined us. I regret to say that all was not rosy in our relationships at times. My style of leadership wasn't readily accepted by a few. I would confide in Curtis about the problems, and he would say, "Well, you know what happened to Satan when he got kicked out of heaven? He landed in the choir loft!" His attempt at humor didn't make me feel any better.

The praise team went down to Parchman to minister in music to the inmates one time. I dreaded the trip because one person on the team had "ought" against me (Matthew 5:23). I had tried everything I knew to make things right between us. Actually, there was no basis for her resentment. I had to continually forgive her for the obvious grudge she held against me. I didn't say anything to Curtis about the dread I had in making the trip. Just as I was stepping into the van, Curtis came hurrying to me with a piece of paper in his hand. After I sat down in the van I looked at the paper. He had written, "To Nancy from Jesus – Job 16:19." What? Was this addressing my problem? I looked it up in my Bible. With much anguish Job replied to his accusing friends: "Surely even now my witness is in heaven, and my evidence is on high." Wow! What a perfect word from God about my situation. I immediately felt vindicated. God had seen everything, and He knew I had done nothing to deserve this person's resentment. How thankful I was that Curtis heard from God on my behalf and passed His message on to me, even though he didn't understand what it meant. As you can guess, this musical outreach to Parchman was a great success! I led the music with joy and renewed confidence.

Curtis and I had a constant disagreement about the sound. He always said it was too loud. I couldn't be sure if he was right because my hearing was not good, and I could only judge by the sound from the monitors. Another factor was that the praise team was on the stage, and the walls were concave. But it was imperative that the sound be loud enough for us to hear ourselves. Anyway, Curtis didn't want me to be the leader. He thought he could spare me the conflicts that inevitably arise between musicians.

A young man and his wife began visiting the church, Bob and Colleen Meek. Bob had been the worship leader at Evangel Assembly of God. (He also gave Bert lessons on the guitar. Bert developed his talent mostly on his own, however, and became amazingly good!) Bob led worship with his bass guitar. Curtis asked him to be the worship leader in June 1994. I was hurt, but I did my best to cooperate. And the Lord gave me great consolation. At the same time, I had to give up my position as leader of the Praise Team at Trinity, I was asked to lead the March for Jesus in Columbus on June 12, 1994. Wow!

The March for Jesus was a national event for Christians to take to the streets and praise the Lord openly. Trinity Church was eager to get in on the action. Curtis and Ken Linton had gone to Austin, Texas, in June 1992, to a planning conference for the first international march. The marches had begun in England in the

1980s, and the first local march in the USA was in Austin, Texas, in 1989. The first nationwide March for Jesus was on May 23, 1992.

Trinity Church invited Quinett Sherrer, a pioneer in making banners, to conduct a workshop for the art of banner-making in February 1993. Our church was ready to join the international March for Jesus, sporting our new banners, on June 12, 1993. This march brought 1.7 million Christians to the streets in 850 cities across the globe to glorify Christ. And just to think, Curtis and Ken had helped to plan it!

Most of the music for the March for Jesus was written by Graham Kendrick. One of my favorite songs of his that has stood the test of time is "Shine, Jesus, Shine." On June 12, 1994, I had the glorious opportunity to lead the Columbus march, singing "Shine, Jesus, Shine," and it was my wholehearted prayer that Jesus would shine His light through me and through all of us marching for Jesus in our city.

Bob Meek led the music for our first worship service in the new building, August 14, 1994. His background in music performance was outstanding, I learned. While he

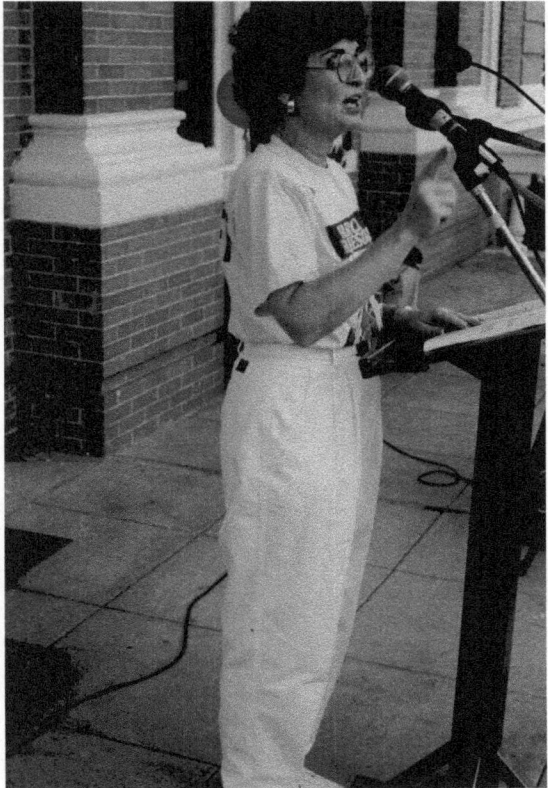

Nancy leading March for Jesus in Columbus, MS, June 1994

Golden Triangle Trinity Church, serving Columbus, Starkville, and West Point, MS

was at Oral Roberts University, he was privileged to perform concerts and take the gospel to Communist countries with Living Sound International, which later became World Compassion Terry Law Ministries. At Trinity, Bob stood right beside the piano to

Trinity Church dedication service, August 28, 1994, Bob Meek and Nancy on the front row

lead the worship. It so happened that many times his voice would give out, and he would motion to me to take over. I was happy to do so, and since it wasn't my responsibility, I enjoyed it even more.

I had it made! Tommy Glenn had purchased a gorgeous grand piano for the new building, and it delighted my soul to play it every Sunday. Bob Meek was a good worship leader, but he was with us only a year. After August 16, 1995, I had my old job back. I was the interim Music Director. Then it was taken away again by our keyboard player, Tim Wilcox. He became our Music and Youth Director in January 1996. Like Bob, Tim was a good leader, too. I had less responsibility, so I couldn't complain. I not only played the piano, but I sang solos, just as I had at the other churches in the past. I was rocking along with impaired hearing, but my hearing loss was not severe. I still had great enjoyment in every aspect of music. Monitors on the stage were not a luxury but a necessity for me, however.

In October 1995, when I was the interim Music Director, I took Margaret Ann Chandler, who was playing the keyboard at that time, and my friend, Esther Troskey, to a Worship Conference at Christ for the Nations Bible Institute in Dallas, Texas. It was helpful to me as the leader of a praise team and as a pianist. There were two highlights of the conference, Martin Nystrom and Dennis Jernigan. In a worship class taught by Martin Nystrom we were privileged to learn piano techniques and also how he wrote the famous praise song, "As the Deer." The other highlight was being in a live recording session with Dennis Jernigan at the piano, leading the students and the conference participants in his newest praise and worship songs. Curtis had already been enjoying Jernigan's taped music ever since he heard his music and testimony at the James Robison Bible Conference in 1986. Dennis had been a homosexual until the Lord set him free. Then he married and had six children! (Curtis and I would later hear Dennis perform in 2015 at The Cove, which is the Billy Graham Training Center in Asheville, NC.)

This Worship Conference was the second conference I attended at Christ for the Nations in Dallas in 1995. The first one was a few months earlier, "Israel in Prophecy" in July 1995. This conference truly changed my life and resulted in a new call from God (see Chapter 29).

# CHAPTER 27

## ACCOMPANYING AND COMPOSING

Our church supported several missionaries. Through Johnny Buckner, a missionary with YWAM from Starkville, MS, we came to know an outstanding Chinese singer, Song Yang. Johnny had met him in China and invited him to come to Mississippi State University as a visiting scholar and stay with Johnny's family. Song Yang brought his wife, Wen Jie, a violinist, and their child, Joseph, with him to the United States in 1993. Through Johnny's witness, Song Yang became a Christian.

"Song" is a perfect name for a singer, and he also had a nickname, the "Pavarotti of China." His credentials were impressive. The world music king, Italian vocalist Luciano Pavarotti, said, "Mr. Song is a distinguished tenor with a great future." He had performed in Beijing, Shanghai, and many other big cities in China. His music was featured on more than 30 television programs or movies, and his tapes were sold everywhere in China. He was Director of the International Cultural Exchange Association in Yunnan, China. He had performed in Tokyo, Hiroshima, Singapore, Thailand, Hong Kong, and Malaysia. After he arrived in the U.S., he sang in Memphis, Chicago, New Orleans, Atlanta, New York, and other cities. Quite impressive.

What a high honor had come to Trinity Church. We would host Song Yang in a Christmas Concert, "O Holy Night," on December 11, 1994. Guess who the accompanist was. Yes, Nancy Petrey had that honor! I accepted the job with great trepidation. Some of the selections were difficult to play and required much practice. At least I knew two of the songs well, "O Holy Night" by Adolphe Adam and "The Lord's Prayer" by Albert Hay Malotte. A few others were familiar, including two from Handel's *Messiah*. I relished a good musical challenge, and I got it! Song and Wen Jie were warmly welcomed by a good-size crowd. Song's tenor voice

Song Yang, accompanied by Nancy - Christmas concert at Trinity Church, 1994

was fabulous, and Wen Jie's violin playing was greatly enjoyed. The concert was a success. They endeared themselves to all of us, and a Christian witness was included in the program with Song Yang's original composition, "Jesus, I Love You."

I didn't hit too many wrong notes, thank the Lord. Now that the concert was behind me, I could rest easy, or so I thought. It was not to be. In only one week, another big Christmas program was coming up, and my original songs would be featured.

Something new had happened in my musical life. The creative juices were really flowing the third week in October in the Trinity Church offices. Denise Collins, Director of the Children's Ministry, sat down at her typewriter, and in only two days the Lord "poured through her fingers" a complete Christmas play for children (with some teens and adults added). She read her finished product to me. I was moved to laughter and tears. We both agreed that original music was called for. I had written a few songs in the past, so I told Denise I would seek the Lord and see if He would inspire me. I would also look for existing children's songs. That very day, as I left the office, I began to sing in the car, and the words and melody flowed out. Before I got home, I had created a unique song. The words alluded to not-often-quoted verses of Scripture. How had those verses come to my mind? Later I discovered that my song was based on four different verses – Psalm 137:2; Isaiah 11:1; 1 Samuel 16:18; and 2 Samuel 6. Surely this was the Lord's doing. I named it the "Harp Song."

The setting for the song was a group of small petulant angels, stamping their little feet about being left out of the angelic choir who would announce the birth of Jesus to the shepherds. They consulted God, and He told them they could sing, too. They had their little harps, and the dance Denise choreographed for them was delightful.

> *1. I hung my harp on the willow tree 'cause I can't sing.*
> *I hung my harp on the willow tree and folded my wings.*
> *The angels say that my notes are sour and off-key.*
> *I'm just too little to play and sing and dance for Thee.*
> *(Spoken slowly with hesitation):* <u>*God, do You agree?*</u>
> *(Spoken with conviction)* ***And God said –***
>
> *2. "Take your harp off the willow tree and play for Me;*
> *Take your harp off the willow tree and dance for Me.*
> *A shoot sprang up from the stump of Jesse, can't you sing?*
> *A root grew out of the dry ground, won't you dance with Me?"*
>
> *3. "David played his harp for Me and sang to Me;*
> *David brought the Ark home, and he danced for Me.*
> *Come now and play for the Son of David at His birth!*

*Sing and dance 'cause the Father sent His Son to earth!"*

*(Defiantly, slowly): I will take the harp, and I will sing
and dance,
And I will make a joyful* **NOISE! (off-key)**

I wrote five more original songs and scored[23] them. All six of my songs were on paper and recorded in time for the first rehearsal with the children on October 30. The Lord surely did a quick work.

The song I wrote for the chaotic angelic choir practice became the title song of the Christmas play, *Heaven's All A'Stir.* It started off with snatches of the traditional Christmas carols. I found a keyboardist who agreed to record the accompaniment tape for the musical. I told him to give the introduction to this song a stirring, tremolo sound in the upper range and to continue it throughout the carols. The entire feel of the song is suspended animation, like you're out of breath with anticipation.

Denise's plot included the walls of Jericho falling down. She had always believed that God ordered the angels to knock them down. I had fun writing this song and used a boogie beat for the piano and rap-style narrative. It would be titled, "Jericho Stomp!"[24]

(Chorus): *The Jericho Stomp! You could hear it
for miles around!
The Jericho Stomp! Michael went out on the town!
The Jericho Stomp! It made a mighty sound!
The Jericho Stomp! It made the walls fall down!*

*Joshua said, "The battle plans have come from the
Heavenly Chief."
He said, "You just walk it, don't you dare talk it,
Take my Ark around the town, only the trumpets
will sound.
A day at the time, six days in all,*

---

23  Scoring music is the process of transcribing the music onto staff manuscript so other musicians can read and play it.

24  Appendix: *My Song Compositions,* "Jericho Stomp!"

*Seven times on the seventh day."*
*The angels all poised, waitin' for the noise,*
*Came the shout! And they began to sway.*
(Chorus)

"Heaven's All Astir," children's Christmas musical at Trinity, 1994

Denise Collins, script writer and director, with Nancy and Curtis

The "grand premiere" of Trinity's own home-grown musical, *Heaven's All A'Stir,*[25] was a big success. Denise and I praised the Lord and gave Him all the glory!

---

25  Petrey, *Habitation of Honey*, pp. 69-74.

# CHAPTER 28

## SONG WRITING INCREASES

The Lord had blessed me with six original songs for *Heaven's All A'Stir*, so at the end of 1994, my compositions totaled ten. The next year would bring forth more songs. So much happened to me that year of 1995. It was exciting, and I was growing spiritually and musically. That year saw a lot of renewal movements throughout the world, such as the famous Brownsville Revival[26] which was preceded by the Toronto Blessing.[27] At the beginning of 1993, Curtis had received a word for our church: "On your knee in '93, I will open the door in '94, and My church will come alive in '95!" This word started its fulfillment in the prayer meetings that began in Columbus in 1993, both in our church and throughout the city. Lars Enarson, an intercessor from Sweden, had brought his family and come to live in Columbus in 1992, and God used him as a catalyst for prayer.

It was at one of these interdenominational prayer groups that I presented a brand new song God had given me, "Messenger."[28] The words began, *"I am a messenger girl for Messiah Yeshua, His name is Jesus. I'll take His word to the world, but first to the Jews, and where His Spirit leads me ...."* The people acknowledged that this song was truly from the Lord. It so happened that Lars was leading

---

26 The Brownsville Revival (also known as the **Pensacola Outpouring**) was a widely reported Christian revival within the Pentecostal Movement that began on Father's Day, June 18, 1995, at Brownsville Assembly of God in Pensacola, Florida.

27 In January 1994, revival broke out at the Toronto Airport Vineyard Church, pastored by John and Carol Arnott. This ministry that affected many nations was renamed "Catch the Fire Toronto" in 2010.

28 Appendix: *My Song Compositions*, "Messenger," 6

two groups from Columbus on prayer journeys to Israel the next month. The song particularly fit the groups' purpose, and I applied it to my friend, Inez Townsend, who was going. Two months later I applied the song to myself when the Lord called me to be a Mizpah (watchman and witness) for Israel (see Chapter 29).

My next songwriting effort came from a prophecy given to me on June 10, 1995, at a Crusade in West Point, MS. I led the singing from the keyboard and sang a solo, "It's Your Song, Lord" by Sandi Patty. Afterward, the evangelist, Brother Robert Branson, said to me that I had "an intense anointing," and that when I sing, "shackles will fall off people!" He also prophesied that I would be doing a recording of songs the Lord would give me from the study of His Word. **The very next day** the Lord began to give me a song right out of His Word! It was finished in two days. Some of the lyrics were the exact words from John 2:1-11, the story of Jesus changing water into wine at a wedding. I titled it "The Wedding Feast (You are Aged Wine)."[29]

I presented this song at Christian Women's Fellowship, and the song was strongly affirmed as a true message from God. Next, I sang it on the Indian Reservation, thinking that the Indians were the "aged wine" referred to in the lyrics, and that God was going to use them in a big way to usher in a last days revival – *"You are aged wine. I've been saving you a long time. You are aged wine. You are a wonder and a sign. You are aged wine. To everything there is a season and a time. The Bridegroom has had a long fast. He's saved the very best till last!"* After time went by, and I got older, I claimed it for the last generation who will see the coming of the Lord. I prayed I would be like "aged wine" and would live to see this happen and take part in the great harvest of souls.

Two weeks after I completed the song I called Brother Branson and sang it to him. He said it was "revelation," and I should get it copyrighted. So, I did.

The Lord may have had in mind that He would use the song to especially touch one man, Leon Sansing, a former pastor, who was

---

29  Appendix: *My Song Compositions,* "The Wedding Feast," 7

now attending our church with his wife, Ozelle. He had become deathly ill, and a group from our church felt like the Lord was directing us to visit him and pray for his healing. As we gathered around his bed and prayed, believing for his miraculous recovery, that is what happened! The Lord stirred me to sing "The Wedding Feast" to him, and the Holy Spirit came upon him. In a few days he was out of bed, and he went to someone he had a grudge against and made things right. Joy returned to his heart which was now free of unforgiveness and resentment. He lived life with a clear conscience for the next two months, and then Jesus called him home. I was highly honored to have played a part in his physical and spiritual renewal. The family showed their appreciation to me by presenting me with a beautifully framed picture of my song, "The Wedding Feast." I treasure it.

The renewal movement of the 1980s and 1990s is sometimes ridiculed as the "charismatic itch" or "charismania," due to many charismatic Christians going overboard with the gifts of the Spirit. Because of this, prophecy has gotten a bad name. It is true that Christians must seek the Lord for discernment when words of prophecy are given to them, but that doesn't mean that personal prophecy should be rejected outright.

Curtis and I benefited from being in the charismatic movement. My answer to naysayers is in God's Word: "Believe in the LORD your God, and you shall be established; believe His prophets, and you shall prosper" (2 Chronicles 20:20). Also, remember what Paul said, "Do not treat prophesies with contempt" (1 Thessalonians 5:20 NIV). For more study, look at the 14th chapter of 1 Corinthians which outlines how the local congregation should use the gifts of the Spirit in its meetings. Anyway, I was blessed by the prophetic word I received from a minister of the gospel. The result was a new song, and it was a prophetic song!

# CHAPTER 29

## A DUAL CALLING

In the summer of 1995, my song-writing totally changed gears. I had a new calling from the Lord, "Mizpah for Israel." God had been drawing me into this specific ministry for years, but in a prophetic word Curtis supplied a title for me. He called me from the church on August 18, 1995. These were his words: "God said you are a Mizpah for Israel." Curtis wasn't accustomed to saying, "Thus saith the Lord," so I paid careful attention to this declaration. I asked him to clarify, and he couldn't. He only knew what the Lord said, not what it meant. I found out that "Mizpah" means "watchman, watchtower, lookout" or "witness."

It was the preceding year in February that Curtis had signed up six of us from Trinity Church to go to Israel. This had a great impact on me. I knew I had gone back to my roots, but little did I know I would soon be knee-deep in the "Jewish Roots Movement." Sixteen years from the time God (through Curtis) called me that day, I began to write a book, *Jewish Roots Journey: Memoirs of a Mizpah*,[30] and one of the chapters is entitled "Musical Mizpah." My musical activities even from before the time God called me to be a Mizpah for Israel up until August 2011, are chronicled in the book, especially in that chapter. I knew God had not revoked my calling to music ministry, so, evidently, I had a dual role now. I was not just a Mizpah, but a "musical Mizpah."

On my first trip to Israel, I had the opportunity to let my light shine for Jesus in Jerusalem in the Old City. Our tour group was about to begin walking on the Via Dolorosa Street ("way of

---

30 Nancy Petrey, *Jewish Roots Journey: Memoirs of a Mizpah* (Gonzalez, FL: Energion Publications, 2012).

suffering" where Jesus carried His cross) Our friend, Frank Troskey, spoke up and asked the tour guide if I could sing the song by the same name as the street, "Via Dolorosa" by Sandi Patty. What could he say but yes? I sang it a cappella. Part of the song is in Spanish, and a woman in our group said I had pronounced the Spanish perfectly. Only God.

On trips to Israel I had opportunities to join in Jewish dances. In 1994 I danced onstage in the YMCA building with the Tzabarim Folklore Ensemble. Yes, I did. At the end of the program members of the audience were invited to come up and dance with the group. We learned the Hora, the Israeli national dance. As we held hands in a circle and whirled all over the stage, I could almost "feel" my Jewish roots. What fun.

Back home at Trinity Church we had an active Jewish dance team that had formed in 1992. At times I participated in it, both at Trinity and at other churches. The Lord had already begun infusing a love for our Jewish roots in our congregation before I even received my call as a Mizpah for Israel.

The "Israel in Prophecy" conference at Christ for the Nations in Dallas, July 1995, was the single event that most impacted my life as a Mizpah for Israel.[31] The messages were so riveting that I could hardly write down the notes fast enough. Actually, I think I wrote down almost every word that was uttered. That had to be God. When I got back to Trinity Church, I copied my notes, stapled the pages together, and put a stack on a table at the back of the sanctuary. That table became known as "The Israel Table," and it soon was laden down with resources from every facet of Jewish ministry.

At the conference, learning about Martin Luther and his anti-Semitic book horrified me. As I heard more and more of the anti-Semitic history of the church, I was determined to teach others about our Jewish roots. I had a burning desire to speak and impart the love for the Jewish people and Israel that I had received at the conference. Back home at Trinity I began Israel awareness classes

31  Ibid, Chapter 6, "Surely Martin Luther Didn't Say That!"

and a prayer group for Israel. I even taught a modern Hebrew language class. We were very blessed to have outstanding missionaries come to Trinity to speak. Among those in Jewish ministry were Reuven Doron, Roy and Mary Kendall, who had a School of Worship in Jerusalem, Lars Enarson, Dr. Michael Brown, and Gustav and Elsa Scheller of Operation Exodus. To say I was excited about being a Mizpah for Israel was an understatement.

My repertoire of Jewish songs had been growing through listening to tapes and playing and singing Hebrew praise songs on the piano. I was studying the modern Hebrew language intensely in hopes of engaging Jewish people in conversation on my trips to Israel. At Trinity we used some of the Hebrew songs in the worship services, especially when we had Jewish speakers or special celebrations around the Feasts of the Lord. My dual calling as a Musical Mizpah had many avenues of expression.

Six from our church had gone to Israel in 1994 – the Troskeys, the Lintons, Curtis, and I. Again, in September 1996, six people – the Troskeys, Randy Gray, Louis Mutch, Curtis, and I – would be going back to Israel. The first trip was a sightseeing tour. This trip was for missions. We would do ten days of volunteer work in Jerusalem with Christian Friends of Israel and Bridges for Peace. In preparation for the trip I endeavored to teach our group two songs, my song, "Messenger," and "My Only Hope is You" by Keith Lancaster and the A Cappella Company. The latter would have been easy to learn, except that I translated the words into Hebrew! I think I was the only one who mastered it. ☺ The Jewish travel agent from Friendly Planet (funny name) helped me with the Hebrew words. As I talked to him on the phone, I was praying hard that the **name Yeshua** would be a Holy Spirit "bullet" in his heart! The Hebrew words were *"Hatikva sheli rak ata,* **Yeshua,** *hatikva sheli rak ata. Meh hashkem ba boker ahd meochar be laila, hatikva sheli rak ata."* ("My only hope is You, Jesus, my only hope is You. From early in the morning till late at night, my only hope is You.") What an anointed song.

On that trip Esther and I helped in the office of Christian Friends of Israel (CFI). We were working away, when they said to stop and get ready for the Wednesday afternoon devotional time for the staff. I don't know how it happened, but I got the **job** (really the **joy**) of playing the keyboard and leading the worship. It was a glorious time, and I felt the presence of the Holy Spirit as we sang.

At CFI we met a wonderful German woman, Inge Buhs, who had a ministry with Holocaust survivors. One day, Esther and I went with Inge to the nice, new home of Maria and Eli, Russian immigrants, where some survivors were gathered. Inge loved on them and distributed checks from CFI for their needs. The survivors spoke Yiddish. This language was similar to German, making it easy for Inge to communicate with them. Eli could speak some Hebrew, so I talked with him in Hebrew a little bit. He had been an officer in the Russian army, and he was a poet. He showed me some books of poetry he had written. I told him I wrote songs. Can you believe I could say all this in Hebrew? We sang several Hebrew songs together – "Hevenu Shalom Aleichem," "Hatikva," and "Hineh Ma Tov." Then I sang a solo for him in Hebrew. How satisfying. All those hours of learning Hebrew songs and vocabulary was finally paying off.

Back on New Year's Eve in 1995, Curtis and I had attended a service at Evangel Assembly of God and met Roy and Mary Kendall and their children, Chip and Marianne. When we went to Jerusalem in 1996, we were invited to their home for a Shabbat dinner. Roy had just started an around-the-clock Prayer and Praise ministry in a room at the Mt. Zion Hotel, and he enlisted us for a three-hour watch. Curtis was our leader, although he had never claimed to be a singer. Nevertheless, nobody could have done a better job. As soon as we finished singing one song, he would start another one, and he never faltered. We prayed for the peace of Jerusalem and sang praises to the Lord non-stop for three hours!

I'll never forget the worship service our group attended at the King of Kings Assembly in downtown Jerusalem at the YMCA building, the same place I had danced onstage in 1994. The service had already begun as our group walked down to the front of the auditorium and filed in. The praise team was leading the congregation in singing the Shema in Hebrew, a cappella: *"Sh'ma Yisrael, Adonai Eloheinu, Adonai Echad. Baruch shem k'vod malchuto, le'olam, va'ed."* ("Hear, O Israel, the Lord our God, the Lord is One. Blessed be His glorious name Whose kingdom is forever and ever.") Oh, the glory of it! The natural voices were like a mighty pipe organ bursting forth with deep passion. How holy is our God. We were standing on holy ground. This Holy Spirit experience was the highlight of the whole mission trip for me.

My third trip to Israel, February 3-22, 1998, was a solo trip. Trinity Church fully supported me and gave me a grand send-off. Some of the ladies had decorated jackets for the Holocaust survivors which would be distributed through Christian Friends of Israel. On this trip I would have three hosts, Roy & Mary Kendall, Mark & Michelle Simon in Jerusalem, and Lars & Harriet Enarson in Haifa. Roy and Mary had just been at Trinity to lead the praise and worship on Sunday morning, December 27-28, and had stayed in our home.

This would be the second time for me to do volunteer work at CFI. They remembered that I had led the worship at the office devotional time in 1996, and they asked me to do it again. As we were singing "I Will Come and Bow Down" by Martin Nystrom, that sweet anointing of the Holy Spirit spread over me, and I had holy goose bumps! The presence of the Lord was such a blessing. "I will come and bow down at Your feet, Lord Jesus. In Your presence is fullness of joy. There is nothing, there is no one who compares with You. I take pleasure in worshiping You, Lord." Indeed, there was great pleasure in worshiping the Lord in His Holy City of Jerusalem with those wonderful Christian volunteers.

# CHAPTER 30

## A TIME OF TRANSITION

Alongside the excitement of my Mizpah ministry and music ministry in the years of 1996 to 1998, there were important things going on in our family. Jim got married to Tricia Hayes in 1996; Curtis had bypass heart surgery on September 10, 1997; his mother, our beloved "Mama Susie," died a month later; and two months after that Curtis went on a mission trip to Cuba in December. Curtis was still fruitful for the Lord post-heart surgery.

My hearing had continued its slow downward progress as hearing tests showed, especially in the left ear. On August 1, 1997, I purchased a hearing aid for the left ear. Still, I had normal hearing in the high frequencies in my right ear, so my music ministry continued. I thanked God for what I **did** have and continued to let my light shine for Him.

A group from Tuscaloosa, Alabama, approached Curtis about coming to be their preacher. He had preached for them on March 1, 1998 and, in a few weeks, they came to him with a formal invitation to be their pastor. Curtis and I began traveling to Tuscaloosa to lead their Sunday evening services on May 7th. I had a new assignment as the praise and worship leader the second Sunday after that. Denise went with us to help me sing as I played the keyboard.

Curtis believed that God was calling him to leave Trinity Church and move to Tuscaloosa to plant a new church which would be known as Christ Church. That August, Curtis announced to Trinity that he would no longer be their pastor by January 1, 1999.

After we moved and began to pastor Christ Church, we heard there was some trouble with Trinity's new pastor, and some of the members had left. Curtis was asked to come back, but the new pastor was firmly entrenched, and it could not happen. The next best thing was for Curtis to drive back to Columbus on Sunday nights and lead worship services for those who had left Trinity. Agape Fellowship was formed on September 1, 1999, and it lived up to its name. Every time we drove over there we had a love feast. These dear friends had been some of the top leaders at Trinity. Now I had become the worship leader for two churches, Christ Church on Sunday mornings and Agape Fellowship on Sunday nights. There was more music ministry at Agape, as I directed the children's choir. I also taught a children's class there. My Mizpah ministry continued at Christ Church, teaching them about our Jewish roots. To add to that, I began working toward a degree in Jewish studies by correspondence from Arkansas Institute for Holy Land Studies.

We had only been at Christ Church for a year and a-half, when Curtis felt it was time for him to retire. On June 30, 2000, we moved into Curtis' childhood home in Petrey, Alabama, and began to attend Petrey United Methodist Church, a very small church that Curtis grew up in. I was the church pianist, and Pastor Davis asked me to sing a solo almost every Sunday. I also taught the only Sunday School class. We were members there for four years. Near the end of our time at Petrey UMC one of the members, Laura Elliott, shared something with me after church. She said that at Thanksgiving when she and her grandson Blake were talking, she asked him what he was thankful for. He said, "The preacher and **the preacher lady who sings and plays the piano.**" What a compliment, especially coming from a young child.

Very soon after we had moved back home, I visited the nursing home (Luverne Health and Rehabilitation) and asked if I could come every week and have a devotional time with the residents, including singing. The Activities Director was glad to have me come. This was something I had done in other places, and it had proved beneficial both for me and for the residents. I could feel the anointing of the Holy Spirit as I taught from God's Word and sang. After I had done this for some time, Curtis began to do the same thing. We were invited by Ann Grier each year to give the Christmas program with Curtis preaching and me singing. Whenever the grandchildren visited us, I would take them and include them in the program. It was a great blessing to make friends with the residents, but it was sad when my favorites died off through the years.

Susan and son, Zachary Zwerg, helping Nancy with Thanksgiving program at Luverne nursing home, 2003

Curtis was always a visionary. He began thinking of ways to bless our area and remembered Song Yang, the "Pavarotti of China," who had given a concert at Trinity Church in 1994. We contacted him to see if he could come visit us and give another concert. He and his family were happy to come. Curtis arranged for the concert to be at Luverne UMC, certainly a bigger church than Petrey UMC,

Curtis and Nancy with Song Yang & family in Petrey - August 10, 2003

and more people would attend. It would be a family concert, "A Melody from China," on Sunday afternoon, August 10, 2003. By this time Song Yang and Wen Jie had two children – Joseph, 16, and Debbie, 4 ½. Wen Jie and the children all played the violin. We were excited about hosting them in Petrey, and I was delighted to be the accompanist once again.

Curtis and I decided it was time to move our membership to Luverne United Methodist Church, a larger church, the one that I had grown up in. We began attending there on June 13, 2004, and I immediately joined the choir and occasionally sang solos and played the organ as a substitute. My time at LUMC was very blessed and fruitful. The church board made me the chairman of a Lay Witness Mission, which turned out to be a huge blessing for the church. Through my friendship with Karen Thompson in Tuscaloosa and introducing her to LUMC, the church bought her Disciple Kids program. This was a rotational Sunday school program that involved drama, crafts, music, and teaching. The adults were a big part of it. Disciple Kids began in January 2006, and there was much fruit from it. Karen had incorporated in her Genesis and Exodus curriculum the things I had taught her about our Jewish roots. I was surprised she had written a dedication to me on the inside page of the book.

As I did in our Methodist church in Columbus, I continued to be pro-active in opposing the UMC **hierarchy's** increasingly liberal and unbiblical position on abortion and homosexuality. This position was not true of most of our Methodist friends. However, I regretfully came to the conclusion that I could no longer remain a member of the United Methodist Church. Curtis agreed. It was regretful to leave the church of our childhood and young adult life. I would always be grateful for my Methodist heritage and the precious memories of growing up in the Luverne Methodist Church, the place Curtis and I married. We were at St. Luke UMC in Tupelo when Curtis and I were saved and called into the ministry.

It was a much prayed-over decision to leave the UMC, and we were sad to have to leave our good friends there. I had learned that the pianist position was open at South Luverne Baptist Church. In May 2006, Curtis and I began attending there. I applied for the pianist job and was hired. This was a brand new facility with a grand piano and a good sound system. I was delighted to have this opportunity and even get paid for it. Christmas was coming, and there was no choir director. I offered my services as a choir director, so we could have the annual Christmas musical. My offer was accepted. We rehearsed *One Small Child*[32] and presented it in December. I was soaring in the heights with joy, joy, joy! My hearing disability had not hindered me. Oh, how I praised the Lord! Curtis was called on to preach from time to time, and we both taught Sunday school. It was a blessing that we were "on the same page" with our class members, regarding social issues. The Baptist church is strong on missions and reverencing the Word of God. We felt right at home and began to make new friends. Edna Ruth Norsworthy had invited us the first time we visited. We kept coming back, until we finally joined and became official Baptists.

South Luverne Baptist Christmas Choir (2014)

---

32 "One Small Child," created and arranged by Tom Fettke, orchestrated by Russell Mauldin, Word Music.

# CHAPTER 31

## PRAYER TOUR IN ISRAEL

I vowed never to go back to Israel alone after I returned home in 1998, so when I felt the Lord's call to attend Lars Enarson's Passover Prayer Tour in 2002, I looked for traveling companions. I found Mary Jo Morgan and Phyllis Huie, two sisters from Huntsville, Alabama, who, like me, were in Lars' Elijah Prayer Army.

When friends and family learned of my plans, the warnings began to roll in – "It's too dangerous over there right now. Please don't go!" Curtis and I prayed about it, talked about it, prayed about it, and talked about it. Curtis and I vacillated back and forth. Finally, the Lord led me to call Roy Kendall in Jerusalem, and his advice hit home. I had the answer. Roy said that any trip to Israel should be based on God's call and not for any other reason. He gave an example of a lady who planned to go to Israel but backed out at the last minute because of perceived danger in the land. She was in an accident and died right in the good ole USA. Roy said, "If you are in the center of God's will, that is the safest place to be."

Little did we know that our 15-day stay in Israel, March 19-April 3, would take place at the **height** of a record number of suicide bombings and the subsequent response by the Israel Defense Force in Operation Defensive Shield.

Before the prayer tour started, Mary Jo, Phyllis and I had a special surprise. Curtis' great-niece, Jennifer Griffin, the Fox News Correspondent for Jerusalem at that time, led us on a short tour of the Old City, ending at the Western Wall.[33] Later that day Jennifer called us to see if we were okay. Her voice was tense. A suicide

---

33   Petrey, *Jewish Roots Journey: Memoirs of a Mizpah, pp. 67-69.*

bomber had detonated near the Ben Yehuda Walking Mall. It was close to the apartment of her Filipino babysitter, Rose, whose balcony was splattered with blood and glass! We got the report later that three were killed and 57 wounded. That was only the beginning of the suicide bombings in Israel during our stay.

This was a prayer tour, and these events definitely improved our prayer life! Besides praying at sites all over the country, I had opportunities to minister in music. After checking in the Mt. Zion Hotel in Jerusalem, I spotted a grand piano across the lobby. It didn't take me but a minute to get to it and begin playing Hebrew songs. The tour group danced all over the lobby, and we had a great time of rejoicing. A man from Paris, two little girls, and a little boy came over to the piano. They loved the music. The man danced. Then a pastor from Portugal came to the piano also. On another day at the hotel, two little girls came up to me, grinning. I wondered if they were the same ones that had gathered around the piano, and they probably were. They wanted to know my name, and they gave their names. I didn't understand much because of the language barrier and also my hearing loss. However, we clasped hands, and we liked each other! Truly, music is a unifying gift from the Father.

I was called on to lead singing from the keyboard at one of our night sessions in the historic Christ Church in Jerusalem. Our group sang and danced to the lively Hebraic music. Earlier on the tour bus I and another lady took the bus microphones and began to lead some Hebraic songs. A lady named Mary Jernigan was very complimentary of my singing, and she wanted to learn the Hebrew songs I had been leading. She urged me to make a recording of the songs.

# Chapter 32

## God Sent a Sparrow

It was 2002, and it had now been fifteen years since my hearing began to deteriorate. It was getting harder and harder to distinguish the bass notes on my spinet piano. I thought to myself, *Here I am a music major, have been playing the piano since I was five years old, and I only have this little spinet piano to play. The quality is terrible, and I can hardly distinguish the pitches. What I really need is a grand piano, so I can hear the bass notes. This is a need, not a luxury.* I was getting more and more positive feedback from my piano playing and singing solos, which affirmed that God was not through with me in the area of music. I began to pray earnestly about my situation, and I thought I heard God say it was a good idea for me to buy a grand piano. By July 2002, I had become certain God wanted me to have a grand piano.

Curtis and I found a used Kawaii grand, not a baby grand, but a 5'10" gorgeous instrument, which had had only one owner, who directed an orchestra from his piano. Though large, it would fit nicely in our high-ceiling living room. The condition of the piano was like new, and the price was excellent, just $6,800. The only problem was that my husband said we couldn't afford it. I reminded him that he had just paid cash for a car which cost much more than the piano and would not last nearly as long! This caused quite a lot of conflict, but I stood my ground – something unusual for me – insisting that the Lord wanted me to have the piano. Our friend, Esther Troskey, offered to lend us the money. The piano was delivered to our house on September 2, 2002, the day before mine and Curtis' 44th anniversary. I was "one happy camper." In a matter of months, our debt was paid, and I was enjoying playing the piano like never before.

Dedicating the piano to the Lord was the first order of business, so I planned a home concert for 20 people on November 3rd. One of the songs on the program was "His Eye is on the Sparrow."

Nancy, ready for her concert to dedicate her Kawai grand piano to the Lord, August 2002

One day before the concert as I was practicing "His Eye is on the Sparrow," Curtis was sitting right outside on the front porch with his feet propped up, listening. A sparrow flew in the porch and lit on the chair in front of him. He thought, *I wish Nancy could see this.* He watched it a good while, expecting the sparrow to fly off any minute, but the sparrow didn't move. Finally, Curtis' legs began to cramp, and he needed to stand up. He had not moved for a long time because he knew the sparrow would fly off if he did. He stood up anyway, and the sparrow still didn't move. Then he eased over to the sparrow, reached out, and took it in his hand! Amazing!

Curtis walked in the living room, where I was still practicing, and held the sparrow up in front of my face. He said, "His eye is

on the sparrow!" Oooooh! I knew at that moment that God had
sent his little "messenger" to both Curtis and me. God was saying
to me, "I'm watching you. It is my will that you have the piano
and that you have the concert. It's not egotistical." I chuckled as
I thought, *God is also saying to Curtis, "You see, your wife really did
need this piano, and I wanted her to have it."* What sweet vindica-
tion.

In case you think there's a natural explanation for this phe-
nomenon of picking up a sparrow with your hand, take note of
what happened next. Curtis immediately went back outside and
released the sparrow. It was not sick. It was just an ordinary
sparrow in the hands of an extraordinary God. The sparrow flew
away. Mission accomplished. And, of course, God was watching
and must have smiled!

Before this, in the spring of 2001, I was asked to play the piano at the First Baptist Church in Luverne. Our worship services
at Petrey UMC were at 10:00 a.m. This enabled me to leave early
and get to Luverne for the First Baptist morning service. I sang
solos at that church and, on occasion, I led the singing from the
pulpit. It was a blessing to reconnect with the people I had known,
growing up. Not long after I started playing their piano, I noticed
a gold plaque at the right end of the keyboard. I was astounded to
find these words engraved: *"This grand piano willed to Luverne First
Baptist Church by Mrs. Ethel Jones Tankersley (1883-1961), volunteer
choir director for over fifty years, March 1980."* What? I remembered
that she was the choir director there for 50 years. It struck me that
this was the very same piano I had played on in Miss Ethel's studio!
My heart was warmed. Again, I knew that God was watching and
must have smiled.

God communicated His love for me through the piano at
First Baptist and through the tiny sparrow with His message of
affirmation. Oh, what a gracious heavenly Father we have. He
meets our needs, but He also gives us the desires of our hearts. As
time has gone by, and my hearing has deteriorated more, I realize
anew what a gift my Kawai grand piano is. Whereas I once had

many varied pleasures in music – listening to recorded music and concerts, directing choirs, playing piano, and singing – my sole musical pleasure now, outside of singing, is playing my Kawai grand piano. My heart overflows with gratitude to God.

*Mrs. Tankersley's Studio*

# CHAPTER 33

## MINISTRY WITH JANICE

A new chapter opened in my life as a Mizpah the day I met Janice Horowitz Bell from Elba, Alabama. Edna Ruth Norsworthy invited me to attend a ladies' meeting at First Baptist Church in Luverne and hear a Jewish lady give her testimony. This happened only a few days after "9/11," the horrific terrorist attack on the World Trade Center in New York City, so I will always remember the date I met Janice. It was September 17, 2001.

I listened intently as Janice told of her life.[34] What a testimony! I was so impressed with this bold, attractive Jewish woman. I got her e-mail address and began to correspond with her. Eventually, we decided to come together for a joint ministry. My e-mail name at that time was Mizpah Tikvah (watchtower of hope), and Janice thought it would be a good name for our ministry. Our purpose would be to help churches reconnect with their Jewish roots and to enlist individual Christians and churches to pray for the peace of Jerusalem, according to Psalm 122:6. We would offer special presentations of Shabbat and Passover as teaching tools, showing Jesus Christ as the Jewish Messiah.

Our first ministry date happened the very same day my Kawai grand piano was delivered to the house, September 2, 2002. With our husbands, Jack and Curtis, we would give a program at New Ebenezer Baptist Church, six miles south of Elba.

Praying for the peace of Jerusalem was a priority with our ministry. We formed an Israel prayer group at my home on October

---

34 Petrey, *Jewish Roots Journey: Memoirs of a Mizpah*, "Chapter 12. One New Man."

3, 2002. The prayer time was preceded with praise and worship. I had made up a song sheet, and we sang together and worshiped the Lord, as I played the piano. We also danced the *"Hora"* with Janice! Our group met monthly either at my house or Janice's.

Mizpah Tikvah Ministries was getting a solid foundation with this prayer support. Jack and Curtis were supporting us, and now they were going to accompany us to an important conference the very next month in Point Harbor, North Carolina, presented by Ebenezer Emergency Fund-Operation Exodus on October 17-20, 2002.[35] How interesting that our first place of ministry with Mizpah Tikvah was at New **Ebenezer** Baptist Church, and now we were going to attend a conference of the **Ebenezer** Emergency Fund. Two Ebenezers – another God-incidence.

At the Ebenezer conference I had been asked to play the piano. I played "Shaalu Shalom Yerushalayim" (Pray for the Peace of Jerusalem) and "Chariots of Fire." Someone created words to this beautiful tune. The chorus ends with, "Ignite me and make me a chariot of fire!" This was my prayer. Janice and I could see the answer in the Holy Spirit's guidance of our Mizpah Tikvah Ministry. Our "chariots" were about to take off! We began to get numerous speaking engagements in the weeks and months ahead. Singing from my Israel song sheets was always included.

We spoke at Ino Baptist, Janice's church. This huge church out in the middle of nowhere, close to Elba, was fertile ground to plant in because the pastor had a practice of leading a group to Israel every year. I led the congregation in singing the Jewish songs and gave a Bible lesson on our Jewish Roots. Janice told about the Miracle Nation of Israel and gave a Shabbat presentation. At the conclusion Janice taught the congregation to dance the Hora, as I accompanied on the piano with "Hava Nagila" (Let Us Rejoice). It was a good meeting and stirred up a lot of interest.

Probably the biggest meeting we had was a two-day Jewish Roots Seminar at Good News Church in Tupelo, Mississippi, in April 2003. Our friends, Ruth and Bill Kitchens, sponsored us. For

---

35  Ibid, "Chapter 13. In Whose Hearts are the Highways to Zion."

years Ruth and Bill had hosted our church cell group in their home after Curtis and I gave our hearts to Jesus in St. Luke UMC's Lay Witness Mission in 1968. There was a big promotion preceding the seminar. Janice gave her testimony at the church in February, and **we both were interviewed at the local television station, WTVA,** on the Morning Show with Kay Bain two times in March. The second time Alan Becker, who was Jewish, blew his shofar, and I sang two songs from my *Hatikva* recording, "The Lord is Building Jerusalem" and "Up to Jerusalem." Did that make me a television star? Well, no, but it surely gave me a wider audience to let my light shine for Jesus!

Nancy and Alan Becker, appearing on WTVA in Tupelo, April 2003

# CHAPTER 34

## MY FIRST RECORDING

My first recording was entitled *Hatikva* (The Hope),[36] the name of the Israeli national anthem. I had been getting phone calls from Mary Jernigan, the lady I met on the prayer tour in Israel in 2002. She wanted me to make a CD of Hebrew songs she had heard me sing. The next year in February 2003, I took the challenge. A friend of ours, Paul Davis, who had once been a radio engineer, brought his microphones and old-style reel-to-reel tape recorder to the house, and we did the recording of 16 songs almost straight through with hardly a glitch. As I sat at the piano and played and sang, I knew the Lord was empowering me. I wasn't trying to get a perfect recording because my purpose was to use it as a teaching tool for Christians to learn the Hebrew songs. It's a good thing I wasn't striving for perfection because Paul's recorder began to malfunction before we finished the session. I was worried that all the grinding sounds from the reel-to-reel recorder would be on the tape.

With fear and trembling, I listened to the tape to see if the malfunction affected the recording, and if my voice and piano performance was acceptable. Curtis and I evaluated it and decided we might as well continue with the process of duplication, although I was not convinced it was good enough.

---

36 *Hatikva (The Hope)* – 17 songs on CD, piano & voice by Nancy Petrey: The Lord is Building Jerusalem, Up to Jerusalem, Hevenu Shalom Alecheim, It is Good to Praise the Lord, Hodu L'Adonai Ki Tov, All That I Need (My Only Hope), Shaalu Shalom Yerushalayim, Sabbath Prayer, Hineh Ma Tov, Hava Nagila, The Exodus Song, Sh'ma Yisrael, Hatikva, He that Keepeth Israel, In the Shadow of Your Wings, I Rise Up to Worship (tune: Chariots of Fire), and Kol Dodi.

I sent off the reel-to-reel tape to a company to duplicate 100 CDs and 50 cassette tapes to give away and sell. A man at the company amazed me with his ability to "fix" a sour note by talking to me over the phone. He simply used the same note on another verse and exchanged that note for the sour note. Voila! I had helped him find the sour note and the replacement note. All this was done with his equipment, as we talked on the phone. Then he removed the air noise between songs. It turned out to be an excellent recording, almost as good as if it had been done in a studio. Paul really knew what he was doing. All my doubts were gone. Praise the Lord! I was a recording artist at last ☺! Mary Jernigan was overjoyed to get her CD, and she ordered many more. I sold the CDs and tapes at seminars and shared the music in other ways. People genuinely enjoyed the *Hatikva* recording.

The most heart-warming compliments I received from *Hatikva* were from my granddaughters, Taylor, who was 6, and Hannah, who was 4, at the time. Taylor started crying when she listened to it and told her daddy, Jim, that she missed "Mama Nancy." They called me and told me they loved the CD. I asked Taylor why she was crying, and she said through tears, "Because I love you!" Later, Jim asked the girls, "Isn't Elvis Presley the best singer in the whole world?" Taylor said, "No! Mama Nancy is the best singer in the whole world!" Both girls went to sleep listening to my CD every night. There aren't words to express how that blessed me. With fans like Taylor and Hannah, what more satisfaction could I find?

Through this recording, I believed that I was fulfilling my dual role as a Musical Mizpah. I planned to take some CDs and tapes with me the next time I went to Israel. My life thus far as a Mizpah for Israel had been tremendously blessed, especially in the area of music.

My granddaughters - Taylor and Hannah Petrey, December 2003

# CHAPTER 35

## MORE MINISTRY ABROAD

I did take my *Hatikva* CDs to Israel that very year, and Janice Bell went with me. One morning I was praying and asking God about another possible trip to Israel. I realized that Janice, a Jew, had never been to the Jewish state of Israel. That should not be. She **had** to go!

While in prayer I had the idea to call Helena (not her real name) for advice on a travel agent, a good time to go, etc. I knew she had traveled to Israel over 30 times, and she could give me some good ideas. I was shocked to learn in our conversation that she had been asking the Lord who the ladies were that she was to give $10,000 to, according to a prophecy she received. Helena said she would split the money between Janice, her niece, and me, and the four of us would go together right away! What? God was answering my prayer in an awesome way. I couldn't praise Him enough.

As it turned out only Janice and I went. Helena had given us each a check for $3,333.33! This whole story is related in my first book, *Jewish Roots Journey: Memoirs of a Mizpah*, Chapter 15 – "Jerusalem, Here We Come!" Of all my nine trips to Israel, that was the best one, and my telling of it occupies five chapters in the book. During our visit to Lars Enarson's Golan House of Prayer in Katzrin on the Golan Heights I had occasion to play the *Hatikva* CD for a time of worshiping the Lord with our hosts, Stephen and Dawn Tofson. It was such a blessing. Stephen said he was hoping we would have a word from the Lord for them. They were nervous about their proximity to Syria, especially since the IDF had just bombed a terrorist camp inside Syria. The Lord led me to read

Isaiah 17 about the destruction of Damascus. Stephen said that may have been the word they needed.

After Janice and I returned home we continued our Mizpah Tikvah ministry, reporting on our trip to Israel, conducting Passover Seders, and speaking about our Jewish roots. There was always an occasion to include music. At each meeting I would pass out my song sheets of Jewish songs, and everyone would sing. Invariably I would sing the "Sh'ma" *(Hear, O Israel ...)* and another song from my CD, and we would join Janice in dancing the *Hora.* Very satisfying.

In September 2007, Janice and I went back to Israel with our husbands. Our trip in 2003 was designed by us, and this one was also. I thanked the Lord and our son Perry for his gift of free airfare to Israel! Besides blessing his mom and dad, his generosity resulted in a huge blessing for Jack and Janice. They were able to connect with Jewish believers and ministries and their biblical inheritance in the "Land of Milk and Honey."

My next foreign trip was a mission to Venezuela, June 24-July 1, 2006. Members from churches in our area, including South Luverne Baptist, signed up for the trip sponsored by Four Corners Ministries. Each of us was encouraged to prepare for our own ministry in Venezuela. I couldn't think of anything else but music. I prayed, and the idea of playing a ukulele and singing songs in Spanish came to me.

My brother David had inspired me with his ukulele-playing. I ordered a baritone ukulele online, and it arrived in January. It was inexpensive, so I didn't know if it was a good one or not. The first thing to do was to tune it. I had a book to go with it, so I tried to tune it, using the piano notes. It sounded awful. I went across the street to get Don Hermeling's help, since he played the guitar. He worked with it a long time and never could get it tuned. He said one string was dead. I was thoroughly discouraged and figured I had wasted $70. Curtis was upset, too. We didn't know whether to try to sell it, pawn it, or go to a guitar store and see if they could fix it. Curtis had thrown away the box, so I couldn't send it back.

Curtis and Nancy with brother David, playing ukulele at Petrey Reunion 2003

Bert came home after I had gone to bed. According to Curtis, he picked up the ukulele and said, "This thing is an octave too low!" He quickly tuned it and said it was a **good** ukulele. What a surprise the Lord gave me when I woke up the next day. Bert is an excellent guitar player, so his opinion settled my doubts. Curtis agreed it sounded good. I began to work on some simple chords and simple songs. The day before, the situation looked hopeless, but after giving the problem to God, it was solved! God can be trusted when we turn things over to Him.

I bought a tuner and a strap for my ukulele, found the Spanish translation for some songs and practiced the chords until my fingers finally developed calluses (a lot of soreness to begin with). We had a "Mission Recognition Day" at Luverne UMC on May 7, 2006, and I took part in the service by playing my ukulele and singing some praise songs I had learned in Spanish. I used my ukulele to lead singing in other places, such as Lake Haven Assisted Living Home. Having a new skill made me feel good, and I knew that only God could have enabled "an old dog to learn new tricks."

Nancy with baritone ukulele, January 2006

I was asked to write a 40-day devotional booklet for the mission team. The booklets were distributed 40 days before our departure on June 24th. At the "blessing service" at SLBC before our mission team departed to Venezuela, I played the ukulele and sang songs in Spanish. The congregation sang along on some of the songs.

Our team had many trials getting to Venezuela and then getting our luggage after the flight. Many the bags were filled with medicine and other supplies for the poor people. The customs officials at Maracaibo only released six of our 44 bags! Much negotiation went on, as well as prayer meetings, until we finally got all but five supply bags. After the spiritual warfare prayer that night, I sat down in the hotel lobby and began to quietly strum the ukulele and sing praise and worship songs. The team gathered for our devotional time and joining in singing. The presence of God filled the room! We all were blessed. These nightly devotional times were very meaningful, as team members shared what they were experiencing.

The first place we ministered was at an open-air mission church. It was a treat to have the little children run up to us and hug us as soon as we got off the bus. Our leader, Carolyn Gholston, had asked me to speak. I spoke on the "Precious Poor," but I didn't feel anointed and thought I had done poorly. However, a lady came forward to be saved. It must have been the message God wanted.

Each day's ministry was closed out, as we gathered around the bus for show time. Some of our team put on a puppet show from the bus windows. Each evening I played my ukulele and sang the songs in Spanish I had learned – "When the Roll is Called Up Yonder," "Jesus Loves Me," "This is the Day," "Open the Eyes of My Heart Lord," "More Precious," "I Surrender All," and "Sing Unto the Lord a New Song." The team had song sheets and sang along. My vision of having children gather around me because I had played the ukulele was fulfilled! I was surprised to learn that the ukulele was a "star" in Venezuela and that it was built there! They call it a "*quatro*" because of the four strings. I had no idea. Wow! Evidently, I really did hear from the Lord back in January, when I ordered a baritone ukulele from the internet and found Christian praise songs translated in Spanish. It was very satisfying to be able to help with the music ministry in Venezuela and get to love on the kids. Thank You, Lord!

Venezuela "show time" - Nancy leading singing with ukulele, July 2006

# CHAPTER 36

## BLOOM WHERE YOU ARE PLANTED

I became the church pianist for South Luverne Baptist on May 31, 2006 (I am still the pianist in 2018). My first time to direct the choir in the morning service was on October 15th. We sang "Days of Elijah" by Robin Mark, and it was a big hit. We got a standing ovation. I first heard the song on the Passover Prayer Tour in Israel in 2002. Every time I sang it I felt the powerful anointing of the Holy Spirit. The verses are about Elijah, Moses, Ezekiel, and David.

The composer, Robin Mark, wrote the words and the chords of this song after hearing the pastor preach on Ezekiel's valley of dry bones in their early morning worship service. He went to the kitchen of the church and wrote it down in only thirty minutes. Then the congregation sang it at the end of the second service. Amazing! Mark said, "The chorus is the ultimate declaration of hope – Christ's return."[37] God had big plans for this song written in 1995, and it is still being sung worldwide. I had John Ganey blow the shofar as the choir sang the words of the chorus, *"Behold He comes, riding on the clouds, shining like the sun **at the trumpet sound** ... in the year of Jubilee!"* What a rousing song for welcoming the Messiah. I loved it! It is a standard for our choir to this day.

Our pastor, Brother Mike Green, asked me to be the Interim Minister of Music at the end of the year, and I gladly accepted. Of all the music we sang, the most ambitious undertaking was the "Hallelujah Chorus" by George Frederic Handel. We sang it at the end of the Easter service on April 8, 2007. It was thrilling and worth all the hard work. Betty Gillette said it sounded like a

---

37  https://robinmark.com/the-story-behind-days-of-elijah/

100-voice choir! There were many more accolades. I always say, "To God be the glory!"

Leading the congregational singing and directing our excellent choir as the Minister of Music at South Luverne was a sheer joy, but my husband Curtis did not want this to be a permanent position. He kept reminding the music committee of that. The committee searched and found a well-qualified graduate student at Troy University, Laura Aaron. She became our Minister of Music on June 29, 2008. I had been the choir director for almost two years. She and I were the first females to have that position. I had led the congregational singing from the piano and have continued in that way as a substitute to this day.

In July 2006, I was asked by Ann Tate to join a steering committee to form an interdenominational women's ministry in our area. This was an honor and afforded me another way to let my light shine for Jesus. The Crenshaw County Women for Christ emerged, and the first one of many annual women's conferences was scheduled for March 24, 2007, at South Luverne Baptist Church. Our theme was "Bloom Where You are Planted." I would be the director of the Women's Choir. We had rehearsals prior to the conference and were ready to perform a medley – *"We Will Stand/ Take up Your Cross* (my arrangement)"[38] – and the popular song, *"You Raise Me Up."*[39] The choir was a big success.

For comic relief, I wrote two skits for the conference, "Screeech!" and "Minnie Pearl Returns." Melissa Bush and Mary Lynn Holliday starred, and I played the part of Minnie Pearl with a crazy straw hat that Mary Lynn fashioned for me. The skits were uproariously funny, and the following women's conferences included my comedy acts. For the 2009 conference I dreamed up the character of Penny Merle (Minnie Pearl's great-niece) to give her home-spun wisdom, and she appeared for several more conferences. Wild songs and poems for these acts were my creations, and I

---

38  "We Will Stand" by Russ Taff and "Take Up Your Cross" by Ray Bolz
39  "You Raise Me Up" by Brendan Graham and Rolf Lovland, recorded by
    Josh Groban

over-acted to the hilt! No one (except the committee) ever knew whether Minnie or Penny would come visit because she was never listed on the program. It was great fun making my grand entrance each time, saying in a loud southern twang, "Well, HOW-DEEEEE! Ah'm jest so glad ah could be hyar!" I really was learning how to "bloom" where I was planted, since Curtis moved us back home. Notice what a "blooming idiot" I was with my Minnie Pearl hat!

Penny Merle, great-niece of Minnie Pearl, going to the Crenshaw County Women for Christ Conference, March 2010

The steering committee also gave me the job of writing a week's worth of devotionals for the committee prior to each conference. I was blessed to do this, It was a spiritual preparation for all of us. The two songs I directed for the Women's Choir the second year were "O Happy Day" and "Still."[40] In following years, we had other choir directors. Besides the skits, I played specials on the piano to prepare for the Quiet Time part of the program.

---

40  "Still" by Reuben Morgan, arranged by David T. Clydsdale

Penny Merle entertaining women with songs and words of wisdom!

At the 2013 conference my friend, Hannah May from Panama City, (her book inspired the writing of my first book[41]) played her violin with me. Everyone greatly enjoyed it. The year before, she came to see me in Petrey, and we played together in church – "Amazing Grace," "Hava Nagila," and "It is Well with My Soul." We got three standing ovations! Another time she played with me was April 3, 2017, in Donalsonville, Georgia at Friendship UMC. Wayne Worsham had asked me to speak at their Israel Day service. I was about to start with a few Jewish songs, singing from the piano, when Hannah and her husband Greg walked in the sanctuary just in time (they had forgotten the time change). Hannah quickly came onstage with her violin. We had a ball playing together. The congregation loved it!

The women's conferences have become very dear to a great host of women in our area, representing hundreds of churches. I have always considered it a wonderful honor to be a part of planning and carrying out these conferences along with the outstanding women on the steering committee (and also with the help of men in our church). Volunteers from other churches have contributed their efforts, and we have had extraordinary speakers.

These are the doors God opened for me to let my light shine for Jesus in Crenshaw County. To God be the glory!

---

41  Hannah May, *Operation Olive Branch: A Collection of Mysteries Uncovered by a Spiritual Sleuth* (Energion Publications: Gonzalez FL, 2011).

I am also grateful the Lord has given me an even wider circle of music ministry in various places in Alabama and Mississippi since we have moved back home. Some of these divine appointments were with Curtis in revivals, Lay Witness Missions, and Emmaus Walks, some in speaking about our Jewish roots, some with piano

Hannah May and Nancy performing at South Luverne Baptist Church, July 2012

students, and some in special services in my own church and in other places. Ministry in Alabama churches has included Eufaula UMC, Oak Grove UMC (near Troy), Joquin Baptist, Glenwood UMC, Zion's Chapel High School (near Elba), Brantley Word of Life Church, Brantley UMC, Pine Grove UMC in Valley, Wesley Chapel UMC in Enterprise, His Vessel Ministries and other ministries in Montgomery, and Tallassee. Curtis and I ministered in a UMC Lay Witness Mission in Cantonment, FL. Places I have ministered in Mississippi are Antioch UMC at Laurel, churches in Hamilton, Starkville, Anguila, Hurley, Southaven, in various meetings in Columbus, and in Olive Branch at a women's conference. (This is not an exhaustive list!)

I taught piano to several students at the Community Education Building in Luverne and to Keith Hermeling in Petrey. I have played and sung solos at many funerals and weddings in various places and at Veterans Day programs in Luverne. On September 11, 2002, in Turner Park at a Service of Commemoration of the Twin Towers attack I played the electric piano and sang "This is My Country" and "Battle Hymn of the Republic."

I have been furiously blooming where God planted me! What an exciting and busy life!

# CHAPTER 37

## RECORDING ARTIST AND AUTHOR

God blessed me with a second recording, entitled "His Eye is on the Sparrow." This came about from a conversation with our preacher's wife, Lisa Green, on January 20, 2010. During the morning worship service, I had sung a solo, "This Little Child" by Scott Wesley Brown. It was Sanctity of Life Sunday, and I felt the Lord had directed me to sing this song. I got a standing ovation and many compliments afterward. Brother Mike said it was "powerful." When he got up to preach he said, "Miss Nancy is ahead of me in age, but I wish I had half her energy!"

Lisa, Mike's wife, said my piano playing always blessed her. She wanted me to make a piano CD so she could listen to it going to and from work. I felt this was definitely something the Lord wanted me to do, so I called a young man I knew at Troy University, Bryan Seagraves, who was studying Music Industry. Bryan recommended his friend, Jason Sanders. I asked Jason, and he accepted the job to record me playing the piano.

After much prayer and practice, the day came for the recording, May 13, 2010. Jason came to my house with all his equipment, which was the very finest, and set it up in the dining room adjoining the living room where my piano was. I would be playing my own Kawai grand piano, just as I did for the *"Hatikva"* recording. Bryan came along to listen and advise. The session lasted from 10:00 a.m. to 12:20 p.m. I played fourteen pieces – three classical numbers by Chopin, and arrangements of gospel songs and hymns. "Battle Hymn of the Republic" was the final number.[42]

---

42  Song list: "His Eye is on the Sparrow," "Minute Waltz" by Chopin, "Revolutionary Etude" by Chopin, "Fantaisie Impromptu" by Chopin,

What a relief to play all the numbers with very little redoing. No doubt the Holy Spirit was anointing my playing and the recording process. Jason was blown away. This was not what he was expecting from a 70-year-old church pianist! After doing the mixing, he had the master CD ready for me on May 26th. I was anxious to know if it really sounded good. It was too bad I could not evaluate my own recording, due to my increased loss of hearing. I had to depend on others' opinions. Of course, Curtis liked it. I could count on him for support.

My grandson Zach, just having graduated from high school, gave me a positive evaluation also. He had played the French horn in the band, so I trusted his educated opinion. He listened to *"Fantaisie Impromptu"* over and over and said it was as good as a professional!

I ordered 100 CDs from Cass-A-Tapes. They came in on June 23rd, and I began to mail them out to friends and family who had pre-ordered. I sent free copies to the immediate family.

My brother David received his CD two days later and called me to say it was excellent and that he had been greatly blessed listening to it. He was raving about it and said that I played *"Fantaisie Impromptu"* as good as it could be played by anyone. He said that the guy who did the recording did an excellent job and the **quality** was excellent! That was what I was waiting to hear. It was very gratifying to know the quality was good. The Lord surely answered my prayer. David went on to say that he started to listen to the CD as background music, but he had to sit down and **really** listen to it. He said the expression was so good. He had only listened to the first four numbers, and **it really moved him**. I wrote in my journal, "Oh, Lord, that was the best comment of all. Again, You answered my prayer. I asked You to let people be touched by Your Holy Spirit. Thank You for touching my brother." David also said

---

"No One Ever Cared for Me Like Jesus," "Jesus Loves Me" (based on "Clair de Lune"), "As the Deer," "Breathe," "Lamb of God," "Here I am to Worship," "Sweet, Sweet Spirit," "When We All Get to Heaven," "It is Well With My Soul," "Battle Hymn of the Republic."

that he listened to the famous pianist, Vladimir Horowitz play "Fantaisie Impromptu," and he preferred my interpretation, which he thought was more expressive! Wow!

The best compliment of all came from our son, Bert. He said, "I listened to the whole thing now, and I'm going to have to side with Uncle David on this. It's excellent, dang near perfect: sound quality, well-played, song selections, just an all around great CD. Thanks for sharing it with me, and I'll find out what Bob (Bob McLeod, his mentor and guitarist and songwriter) thinks of it soon. Good job!" My heart swelled with gratitude to read Bert's comments.

Lucy Jackson, Curtis' first cousin, called after she listened to the CD. She bought four more copies and said while listening, she had **"an experience with Jesus!"** Later, she bought more and shared them. I continued to get good feedback from the CD, and many people encouraged me to make another recording. Years later, I made an effort to do that, but by then I had more hearing loss, and the recording had only a few good songs on it. Alas! This didn't steal my joy, however, because the two recordings I had made were fulfilling God's purposes. He was the one I wanted most to please. And the comments that meant the most to me were from my family.

Besides playing the piano and singing, the Lord has enabled me to write. He has blessed me with four books besides this one, and the four balance my dual role as a musical Mizpah. The first and third are about the Jewish roots of the Church, our Jewish Messiah, and Israel. The second and fourth contain poems, songs, and devotionals, some of which are about Jewish roots. Songs are featured in all except the third book, and all four are Bible-based. They are full of honey because the Word of God is sweet. *"How sweet are Your words to my taste, sweeter than honey to my mouth"* (Psalm 119:103). Here are my four "honeycombs" in order:

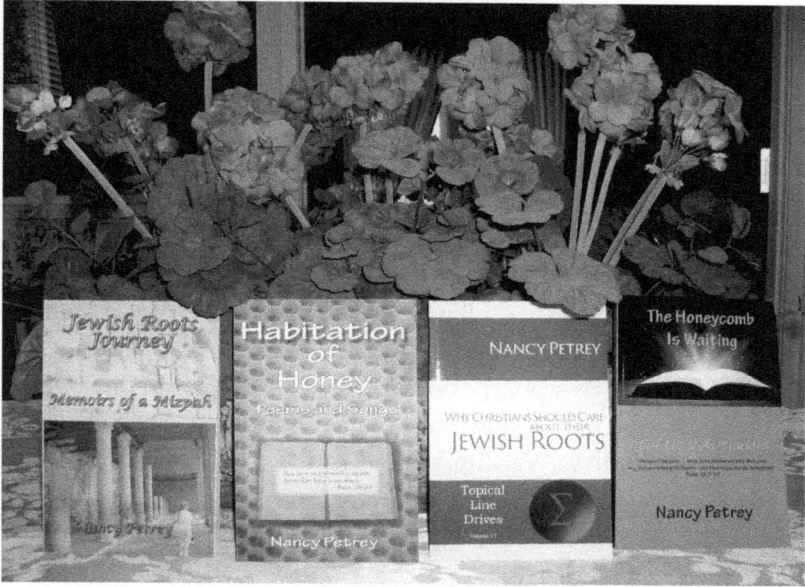

*Jewish Roots Journey: Memoirs of a Mizpah* – 2012
*Habitation of Honey: Poems and Songs* – 2015
*Why Christians Should Care About Their Jewish Roots* – 2015
*The Honeycomb is Waiting: Poetic Devotionals* – 2016

The title song of the fourth book, "The Honeycomb is Waiting," is one of my favorites. One morning as I stood at the bathroom mirror, getting ready for the day, a poem made its way into my mind, as so often happens in the freshness of the morning. It rarely happens, however, that a melody will accompany the poem, but it happened in this case. It was so full of joy, I danced around the room. I could picture my friend, Hannah May, playing her violin to it. The subject was the Bible, likened to a honeycomb. The song begins, *"The Honeycomb is Waiting – why don't you take a bite?"*[43] My goal was to entice people to really devour the Word of God like they would a honeycomb. *"Pleasant words are like a **honeycomb**,*

---

43 Nancy Petrey, *The Honeycomb is Waiting: Poetic Devotionals* (Gonzalez, FL: Energion Publications, 2016), pp. x-xi

*sweetness to the soul and health to the bones"* (Proverbs 16:24). How can anyone turn down benefits like these?

I had hoped this poem would be the signature song of a sequel to my first book of published poetry, "Habitation of Honey: Poems and Songs." My hopes were realized. In the summer of 2016, Janice Bell and I took a Florida trip to visit friends and family. On the way back, we stopped at Hannah May's house. She had arranged a gathering of her friends, so she could introduce them to us. I finally met my publisher, Henry Neufeld, face to face. We had refreshments and visited. Then Hannah told me to read some of my poems from my two poetry books. Next, just as I had envisioned it, Hannah took her violin, I sat down at the piano, and we played "The Honeycomb is Waiting." What fun!

Gathering at Hannah May's house in Lynn Haven, FL, August 2016 - Tulita Owens, Janice Bell (Lewis), Hannah, and Nancy

I am so grateful for Hannah May because it was through her that I first learned of Henry and Jody Neufeld of Energion Publications. Hannah promoted me, and they have published all my books. When your light is shining for Jesus, God always gives you people who will put your light on a lampstand. *"Nor do they light a lamp and put it under a basket, but on a lampstand, and it gives light to all who are in the house"* (Matthew 5:15).

Nancy and Henry Neufeld, my publisher (with wife Jody of Energion Publications) at the gathering

# Chapter 38

## Performance Tips

From the first time I performed in Miss Ethel's piano recital as a first grader, I was terrified of playing by memory. Since I had never played "by ear" at that time, I had only the visual memory of the sheet music to rely on. Thankfully, I made it through each recital, but it was "by the skin of my teeth!" As for **singing** in her recitals, it was not nearly as frightening. Other than the recitals, through the years I most always had the music in front of me when I played, and what a relief that was. Except for Miss Ethel's recitals, I did not sing many solos until I began to sing as a young adult in church choirs. For Christmas and Easter cantatas I would be assigned a solo part at times, but the music was right in front of me. There was no fear, only joy!

After I gave my heart to Jesus, everything changed. "Fill My Cup" was one of the first songs I sang as a real Christian. When I sang solos, people were touched. The Holy Spirit was anointing me. I sang solos in the St. Luke UMC choir and on Lay Witness missions. I was also asked to sing for weddings.

It was more effective to sing a solo from memory, and I noticed that the Holy Spirit anointed my singing much more. At a wedding I learned a good lesson – don't rely on a "cheat sheet." I was singing a solo and had my words on an index card in front of me on the pulpit. During the song I looked down to see some of the words and couldn't find the right place to fix my eyes. I stumbled, and the song didn't go as well as it should have. From then on, I determined to have my song memorized and simply trust Jesus to bring the words to my mind. (I broke my rule a few times, but overall, I kept it.) Jesus never let me down, and the people were blessed.

Getting out of the boat and walking on water like Peter became my mantra. I determined I would do the best preparation I could and then leave it up to the Lord to hold me up. If He didn't hold me up, I would sink. This attitude worked for playing the piano as well. And prayer backup is absolutely essential. Not only did I pray for myself when I had to perform, but I asked at least one other person to back me up in prayer. I had an excellent batting average this way.

Another rule I arrived at, especially for playing the piano by memory, was to never practice on the day of the performance. I would only play through the piece once. I have broken this rule quite a few times, but it is so much better to get all the preparation done way in advance.

Keep going, no matter what. Yes, I learned that from the embarrassing moment I had when my hands froze on the keys on public television at the University of Alabama! (See Chapter 11.) There have been times I forced myself to keep going when I "slaughtered" a passage, determining to play the rest of the piece so well that no one would remember my mistakes. At other times I have made such a bad mistake that it threw me off, and I was unable to continue. In that case I would go back to a place in the music I could begin again. In one performance I did this, and no one was the wiser. This really surprised me. After all these years I am still learning new things. Now I prepare ahead to have those "go-back places" ready, in the event I stumble and can't go on.

I played "Battle Hymn of the Republic" on two Veterans Day programs, November 12, 2017, in the morning at South Luverne Baptist Church and in the afternoon at Luverne United Methodist Church Dei Center. I played it by memory as I had done in public successfully several times before. However, in both **these** performances I could hardly get off the ground! I hit the wrong notes on the first few measures each time. It unsettled me, but I kept going, playing with all my heart. As it turned out, I had more accolades on these two performances than on any others. I was so grateful to the Lord. Evidently, He had "covered for me," so that

the audiences could hear the music correctly in all its glory! Yes, to
God be the glory!

One of the ways to practice hard passages is to play them very,
very slowly. This takes a lot of discipline to "hold your horses."
For runs, accent the first note of each four 16th notes, for instance.
You develop "muscle memory." What an amazing ability the Lord
gives us to play very difficult pieces by memory. Continual practice,
using the same fingering, gives you "muscle memory."

After 73 years at the keyboard I still do not have a perfect
grasp of the chord structure of the pieces I play. It is imperative
that a pianist know how to find the tonic chord of the key, should
you "get lost" in a performance and have to end it. After playing
certain pieces for decades, sometimes I shock myself by not even
remembering what key these pieces are in. Please don't gossip about
the skeletons in my closet! Ha! Ha!

When you are playing for the Lord's pleasure and for the ed-
ifying of His people, you will invariably be attacked by Satan. He
is jealous of you because he was once the worship leader in heav-
en and got kicked out. His pride and rebellion to "be like the
Most High" was his downfall. When I led worship from the piano
at Faith UMC, he attacked me many times with a spirit of con-
demnation. I would imagine negative criticism from people in the
congregation as I sang and played. This was spiritual warfare. Satan
didn't want me or anyone else to be blessed. I needed a weapon.
The Lord supplied me with one – *"You prepare a **table** before me
in the presence of my enemies ... "* (Psalm 23:5). **My piano was my
table!** It was my weapon and my provision, on which I and others
could be spiritually fed.

This spiritual warfare continues to the present day but has
become less severe. Anyway, what man thinks is not important.
What God thinks is what matters. *"The fear of man brings a snare,
but whoever trusts in the LORD shall be safe"* (Proverbs 29:25). It is
easy to imagine that people in the congregation are thinking, "Oh,
she is just showing off," or something critical like that. I must
remember that God has said, *"Let your light so shine before men,*

*that they may see your good works and glorify your Father in heaven"* (Matthew 5:16). And I do give Him the glory.

When I stop to think about how many people are responsible for the display of my God-given talent in playing the piano, it is mind-boggling. There is no room for pride, only for humble gratitude. Let me list some of the main ones I am grateful for: my grandmother, Ada Marley, my mother, Nan Williams, my teachers – Mrs. Ethel Tankersley, Miss Virginia Stiles, and Mrs. Amanda Penick – Thomas Piano Company, those who crafted my Kawaii grand piano, the myriad of composers and music publishers whose music I play, and the inventor of the piano, Bartolomeo Cristofori! This is a short list. "No man is an island."[44] My most heartfelt thanks, however, goes to the Lord Jesus Christ, my Creator and my inspiration.

---

44  Quotation from John Donne (1572-1631). It appears in *Devotions upon emergent occasions and several steps in my sickness - Meditation XVII*, 1624

# CHAPTER 39

## MY HEARING DISABILITY

When I lapse into complaining about my hearing loss, I am often reminded by someone that Ludwig van Beethoven, a German piano virtuoso and one of the most famous and influential of all the world's composers, became deaf and yet continued to compose music, play the piano, and even direct the orchestra. My hearing loss began when I was 48, but it was in his late 20s that Beethoven's hearing began to deteriorate. By the age of 44, Beethoven was almost totally deaf. This was in 1824, and at the end of the premiere of his *Ninth Symphony*, he had to be turned around to see the tumultuous applause of the audience because he could hear neither it nor the orchestra! A few years before this he had given up conducting and performing in public but had continued to compose. Many of his most admired works came from the last 15 years of his life. He was only 56 when he died. Unlike Beethoven, I have retained enough hearing to function musically to a surprisingly great degree, especially considering that I am now 78 years old.

I suppose the only comparison that could be made between Beethoven and me is our being pianists and suffering from hearing loss and tinnitus. The tinnitus I have could be described more like the air noise you hear in an airplane. It is not a high-pitched, shrill sound, thank the Lord. Beethoven's tinnitus was most severe, and that could have accounted for his thoughts of suicide at times. When the tinnitus began (see Chapter 22), I felt like it was "blocking" or "competing" with what I needed to hear. But as time went on I didn't even notice it. It is always there, but I am not aware of it, unless I purposely listen for it. That is a blessing.

At the beginning my hearing tests showed a hearing loss in both ears in the low frequencies, especially in the left ear. The hearing aid for the left ear that I bought in 1997 was all I needed until the hearing in my right ear began to decline about eleven years later. I visited the AUM (Auburn University at Montgomery) Speech and Hearing Center and purchased two Resound hearing aids, receiving them on November 14, 2008. They were wonderful, and I was encouraged. I only had them a month, however, when I decided I really did not need the right hearing aid and returned it. Unfortunately, eight months later the hearing in my right ear in the high frequencies took a dive! I could feel it the moment it happened. It was in August 2009. I went back to AUM and purchased the right hearing aid again. I learned to adapt, and things were better overall.

I could continue playing the piano, singing solos, and singing in the choir, amazingly! The very hardest thing for me, however, was and is conversation. My latest hearing tests show that my hearing has dropped in all frequencies. In other words, the hearing loss is across the board. One-on-one in quiet surroundings is doable, unless the person I am talking to has a low and/or soft voice. Projecting your voice and enunciating clearly is the way to converse with a hearing-impaired person. If only people understood this. Sometimes when I ask a person to talk slower and a little louder, it is as if I had not asked them, so I get frustrated. Almost everyone who is unfamiliar with hearing problems thinks that turning up the volume is the answer, but it isn't. There is more involved, at least in the kind of disability I have.

Having conversation in a group is another ballgame, and I rarely win the game. It can get depressing. I miss all the punchlines to jokes and stories because the storyteller usually laughs when delivering the punch, and that overrides the words for me! (When preachers deliver their "punchlines," they often lower their voices to an intimate level for their profound final sentence. Alas!) Something I have learned in a group is when I see that I am not even getting the subject, I ask a question directly, "What did you say?"

Or I may ask the person next to me, "What did he say?" I do better when I am more assertive instead of suffering in silence. My hearing is worst at the end of the day or when I am really tired. But for comic relief, I sometimes interject choice comments just to see if I am anywhere near what the conversation is about. It's all about participation, right? So, we "deaf" people should go for it! I have a good example in my friend, Jane Davis, who is completely deaf. She lip reads, and her husband helps her by making a few hand motions to get her on track sometimes. Jane does not allow her disability to keep her from having conversations. She is pro-active and reaches out to people. The tendency to withdraw is something I have to guard against when I am feeling "in the dark," but Jane perseveres. She is a real inspiration to me.

Watching television can be a great blessing because most programs and movies have captions these days. There is no straining to hear. I can just relax, provided I find something uplifting, something other than the 24/7 news programs. Of course, I can't watch musical programs or go to live concerts. I remember one glorious exception, however. Curtis and I celebrated our 50th wedding anniversary, taking David (my brother) and Mary with us, and joining a tour of three cities in Central Europe. In Vienna we attended a Mozart & Strauss concert by the Vienna Chamber Orchestra in the Auersperg Palace, where Wolfgang Amadeus Mozart himself had performed. Our guide had connections. We arrived at the start time and entered the auditorium. It was packed with people who stared at us as we walked quickly down the aisle to the very front row, the only vacant seats! We were so close to the stage that I could reach out and touch it. A female violinist conducted the orchestra. Wonder of wonders, I could "comprehend" the beautiful music of violins, violas, string basses, and woodwinds, and I thoroughly enjoyed myself. Surely the Author of music had arranged this concert with me in mind! My heart was full of worship.

Live music from natural instruments is kinder to my ears. Recorded or electronic music is the hardest for me to comprehend. I rarely listen to music coming through the television or from CDs in the car. Most of it sounds distorted to me, even my own CD recordings! Praise the Lord that I can still enjoy my piano as I play it, and I can still sing all day long and love it. The accompaniment CDs we use in the church choir are of no use to me. I can't "comprehend" them. I have to depend on the singer next to me to come in on time and to be on the right pitch. When I am firmly rooted in a certain key, I can sing the music correctly. But if a particular piece changes keys often, I get "lost." Another strange thing is how I perceive the men's voices. For instance, one time I was enjoying the men's voices as they sang alone. Their music was so beautiful. Then it was time for the women to join in, and I confidently opened my mouth and sang. Unfortunately, although I was singing just fine, I was in the wrong key! How could that be? My ear had picked up the wrong frequency, evidently. My confidence was being destroyed, and I didn't trust myself to sing on key any more. This was very humbling because I was the "expert," you know. In the choir my taking a solo part with a CD accompaniment was no longer an option. The last solo part I had in the choir was for the Christmas music in 2011. I was singing my heart out in the choir room during the practice, only to find out from Evan, our director, that I was "sharp." This was another humbling experience. I made the decision to give up the solo, but I stayed in the choir for the presentation of that Christmas musical and have continued to participate in our church choir.

I was not totally denied solos, however. As long as I played for myself, I could stay on key. In the past I preferred to sing with CD accompaniment and only occasionally sang from the piano. All that has changed. As recently as August 6, 2017, I sang and played "The Lord is my Light," a victorious song to the words of Psalm 27 and music by Frances Allitsen. I got a standing ovation!

Part of my job as church pianist is to play the electric piano in the choir room for rehearsing the voice parts at our weekly practice time. I probably would have resigned from the choir already if not for that aspect of my job.

A good friend at church, Morris Tate, told me about his search for good hearing aids. I advised him to go to AUM, and he bought some expensive Phonak hearing aids. One of my greatest hearing needs was to be able to hear the prayer requests in our small Sunday school room and also the prayer requests coming from all over the large auditorium at the Wednesday night services. Morris told me he could hear them clearly with his new Phonak aids. I was greatly encouraged by all the good things he said about his purchase. I determined to go back to AUM and replace my Resound aids with aids by Phonak. In desperation I "bit the bullet" and paid $6,000 for a set of Phonak aids on January 12, 2015. I was told they are wireless, "talk to each other," and automatically adjust to every hearing environment. This was good news.

They did not work a miracle for me, unfortunately. Two sweet ladies, Morris' wife Ann or Debra Little, now sit with me on Wednesday nights and write down the prayer requests. I am grateful for their help. These new aids are better, and life goes on. I praise the Lord for my hearing aids, and that I had the money to pay for them. Here are some audiograms that compare normal hearing with the audiogram of my hearing, tested on March 1, 2018.

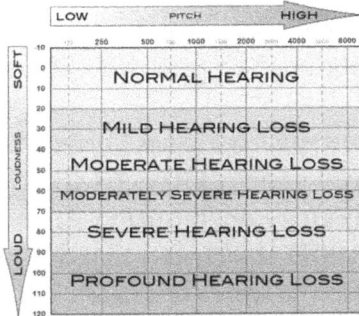

Audiogram chart showing degrees of hearing loss

I have a moderate to severe hearing loss, but it is not a profound hearing loss, praise the Lord!

I recall often what Dr. Wilton McRae in Troy told me years ago, "You will not ever go deaf." And I know it is true. What about divine healing? I do believe I have experienced God's healing, or otherwise I would have gone deaf. My main prayer after I got the first hearing diagnosis was, "Lord, please let my hearing stabilize and not drop any further." For years it remained steady, but since 2008, the hearing loss has progressed. I have prayed for

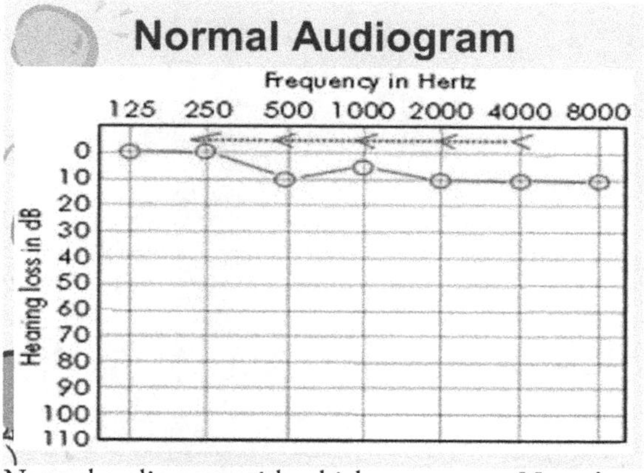

Normal audiogram with which to compare Nancy's hearing loss

myself fervently, claiming every healing Scripture, and I have done all I know to do, including using natural means. I have received prayer for healing numerous times, including hands-on prayer from Bill Johnson[45] at a Healing Conference at CFNI in Dallas a few years ago. I still believe God will heal me either here or in the hereafter.

One of my heroes is Heather Whitestone, who became Miss Alabama in 1994 and in 1995 became the first deaf Miss America! The most astounding thing about Heather is what she did in the talent segment of the pageant. Her ballet interpretation of Sandi Patty's "Via Dolorosa" drew repeated ovations from her spellbound audience as she danced to music she could not hear![46] We know that with God all things are possible. In her devotional book, *Believing the Promise,* Heather summarizes her inspiration and motivation for not only competing in Miss America, but for living out her everyday life. She wrote, "My answer can be summed up in this verse, Matthew 6:33, *'But seek ye first the kingdom of God, and his righteousness, and all these things shall be added unto you.'*" On a much smaller scale I hope I, too, can be an inspiration to others

45 Bill Johnson is a charismatic Christian revivalist, itinerant speaker, author, and a Senior Pastor of Bethel Church in Redding, California. He is a 5th generation pastor. In 1998, Bill and wife Benji started Bethel School of Supernatural Ministry to train up a generation that walks in "revival culture."

46 www.youtube.com/watch?v=9oh7mH7soZU

Nancy Petrey
Patient Id: 366
Age: 78 years, Female
Birthdate: 11/28/1939
Reliability: Good

GSI 61 Clinical Audiometer, 20000243
Calibrated:
Test Date: 3/1/2018

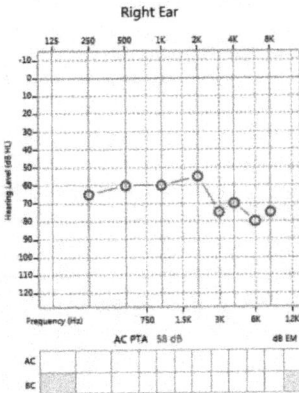

### Right Ear

### Left Ear

| | Symbol Key | | |
|---|---|---|---|
| | | Right | Both | Left |
| AC Unmasked | O | | X |
| AC Masked | Δ | | □ |
| AC NR | ᗡ | | ⋊ |
| BC Unmasked | < | | > |
| BC Masked | [ | | ] |
| BC Forehead Masked | ˥ | | ˥ |
| BC Forehead Unmasked | | ∨ | |
| BC NR | ᒕ | | ᒐ |
| Sound Field | S | | S |
| Sound Field Aided | A | | A |
| MCL | M | M | M |
| UCL | U | U | U |
| TEN | TEN | | TEN |

REF: ANSI S3.6 / IEC 60645-1

AC PTA  58 dB                    dB EM

AC PTA  50 dB                    dB EM

| | AC | | | | | | | |
|---|---|---|---|---|---|---|---|---|
| | BC | | | | | | | |

| | AC | | | | | | | |
|---|---|---|---|---|---|---|---|---|
| | BC | | | | | | | |

### Speech Test Results

### Speech Test Results

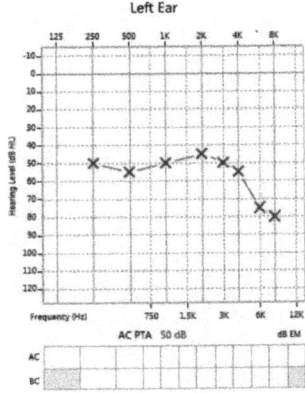

| Ear | Test Type | Int Ext Mic | Word List | Aided | % | dB HL | db EM | Ear | Test Type | Int Ext Mic | Word List | Aided | % | dB HL | db EM |
|---|---|---|---|---|---|---|---|---|---|---|---|---|---|---|---|
| Right | SRT | Mic | | | | 55 | | Left | SRT | Mic | | | | 55 | |
| Right | WRS | Int | w22 | | 72 | 85 | | Left | WRS | Int | w22 | | 76 | 85 | |

QuickSIN SNR Right 0                    QuickSIN SNR Binaural 0                    QuickSIN SNR Left 0

Comments:

Nancy's personal audiogram on March 1, 2018

around me, letting my light shine in the musical gifts God has blessed me with, despite my hearing disability.

# CHAPTER 40

## MY PROMOTER HUSBAND

My musical talent came from both sides of my family. Curtis didn't have that blessing, but he received a huge deposit of wisdom in many fields, besides his phenomenal gift of preaching. Nevertheless, Curtis had the distinction of being the only one among all our family members, in addition to everyone from miles around, of playing the piano in Carnegie Hall in New York City! This happened on his high school senior trip in the summer of 1957. Jack Knowles, who hailed from Petrey and was then living in New York, had a key to the building! He let Curtis' group in. Jack said Carnegie Hall had the most amazing acoustics, that even a whisper onstage could be heard in the far reaches of the auditorium. Curtis was sent to the stage to play the big grand piano, while the others stood far away in the balcony. The acoustics would be tested by his performance on the piano. Luckily, he knew the first few chords of "Chopsticks," and that is what he played. Thunderous applause followed his magnificent musical display of talent! All had a good laugh, and Jack's claim was proven.

Curtis had faithfully attended my recitals when we were going steady in high school. In college he sat with me through many a boring concert. After we married, he patiently endured my practice on the piano and other instruments in our apartment. He survived all the vocalizing I had to do as a choral music teacher to prepare for my classes and concerts. Curtis was rewarded for sticking it out when he was called to preach. His wife became his personal church pianist and song leader. She could carry out his wishes for certain music at certain times, as the Lord was directing him.

After Curtis retired from being a pastor, and we moved back to his childhood home in Petrey, we each had our pleasure domains. Mine was in the living room, playing the piano and singing. His was in the den in a comfortable recliner, watching sports on T.V. to his heart's content, especially the Alabama Crimson Tide games. There was little interaction between us when we were "doing our own thing." I did not realize how proud he was of my musical talent, but I should have guessed it.

Every time someone came to the house to visit, Curtis would invariably invite them to come to the living room and sit. This was the routine after enjoying a big meal I had prepared (with not much help from Curtis). When we were comfortably seated, Curtis would say to me, "Nancy, play 'Rainbows.'" I would usually say, "You mean 'Fantaisie Impromptu' by Chopin." Then I would protest and say I had not practiced it lately, but I would try. I would think to myself, *Why does he always ask me to play when I am so tired?* More times than not, however, I would play it with few mistakes, and we all enjoyed it. I knew it was the grace of God. I finally realized though, that I better practice beforehand when we had dinner guests scheduled. Whatever Curtis asked me to play, I made a valiant effort to do it. His favorites, besides the Chopin number, were "I Rise Up to Worship" (tune: "Chariots of Fire") and "Jesus Loves Me" (based on "Clair de Lune"). More than once he requested I play and sing the "Chariots of Fire" song at church. All these are on my CDs.

Unbeknownst to me, Curtis had bigger plans for me than playing the piano at home. He was going to make me a concert pianist! Curtis served on the American Family Association (AFA)[47] board for over 25 years. From 2012 to 2016, AFA sponsored a retreat for their supporters at The Cove – The Billy Graham Training Center in Asheville, North Carolina. Curtis and I attended three of the retreats, and I attended the 2016 retreat as a widow.

At the first one we attended in the fall of 2013, **I had a huge surprise from the Lord, a Holy Spirit experience playing the**

---

47   http://www.afa.net/who-we-are/our-mission/

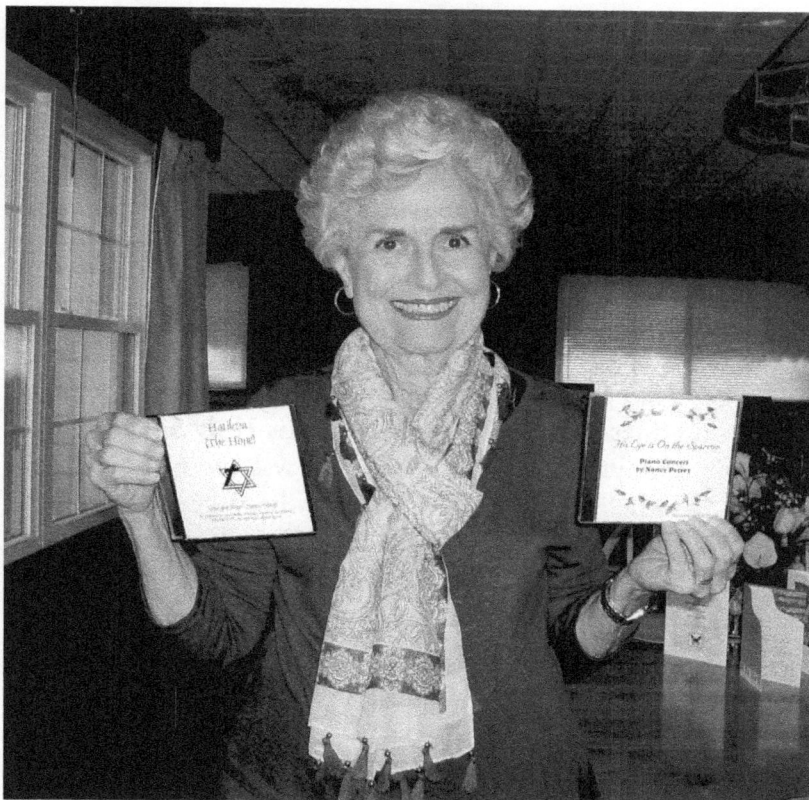

Nancy's two CDs - "Hatikva" and "His Eye is on the Sparrow"

**piano onstage to 300 people from 27 states!** Curtis insisted I play "Rainbows." I had not played it in so long, and the idea that I may make a big mess of it just terrified me. Curtis wouldn't let me beg off. He arranged my performance with staff members. I found some time to practice, but my fears didn't go away. I hardly slept the night before. "How would this fit in with the program, and what purpose would it fulfill?" I protested. I emailed Susan an S.O.S. for prayer help. All night I quoted Bible verses and words to songs and hymns. Still I couldn't FEEL God's presence or get any confidence that I would play well.

It was decided that I would play the piece as a "prelude" to the morning session of the last day. I was grateful it was morning because I would be able to hear better, and I was fresher. Also, I could go ahead and get it over with and enjoy the rest of the day. They had me begin playing at 9:30 a.m. The spotlight came on. People were still arriving, but it got quiet. Curtis told the sound man to make sure I could hear the piano in the monitor, alleviating one of my worries. I played away and only made a mistake at the beginning and one at the end, which was not too noticeable, I hoped. When I finished, I got thunderous applause, and people in the back of the auditorium were standing up, clapping! I smiled, bowed, pointed up to the Lord, giving Him the glory, and sat down. I was overcome at the good reception and that **the Lord had seen me through, as He always does. He anointed me with His Holy Spirit.**

The AFA President, Tim Wildmon, was the master of ceremonies, and he promoted my CDs. All who were interested in a CD would have to see me after the session. People crowded around me to order my CD, "His Eye is on the Sparrow," which has three classical numbers on it, including the one I played. Later, when we toured the chapel, Curtis made me play the piano in the sanctuary. He told me to play and sing "Chariots of Fire" ("I Rise Up to Worship"), and I did, in a relaxed manner, looking out at the audience. I really enjoyed it. We met Edgar and Edith Rowand from Kentucky. Edgar said when I played the Chopin number he worshiped! And as he was telling me that, he cried.

The experience of playing "Fantaisie Impromptu" on a beautiful black Yamaha grand piano for that many people was just glorious. All the suffering beforehand was worth it! I especially valued the expressions of gratitude from many, saying my performance was "a gift." Some of the ladies were piano teachers and were so grateful for this music. I was lavished with love and praise, and I passed it on to the Father. Curtis said I have a great talent and should not hide it under a bushel. I thanked my wonderful husband for promoting me.

At The Cove the next year, 2014, Curtis insisted I play again. I did a repeat performance of Chopin's "Fantaisie Impromptu" at the afternoon session of the second day. Then Curtis insisted I play at the evening session that night, "I Rise Up to Worship (Chariots of Fire)." He was really promoting his wife. It was the same as the year before – I didn't have any notice of my part on the program until it happened. I got two standing ovations and sold CDs and books again. People complimented me profusely and sincerely over and over!

Our third time at The Cove in the fall of 2015, I was ready. I had put in a lot of practice on several numbers, but I told Curtis to please not say anything to Tim. People asked me if I was going to play again. Several of them who heard me play the year before implored Tim to let me play, I learned later. Curtis and I were sitting there, and I was wondering if I would be asked, and if I was asked, what piece I would play. I prayed hard. When Tim called me to the stage and introduced me, suddenly I knew what to play, "Revolutionary Etude" by Chopin. Due to the turmoil in our country and the raging culture war that AFA was deeply involved in, I was confident this piano piece fit the program. I stood by the piano and said, **"We need a revolution of righteousness and the gospel in our nation!"** Then I ripped into the music. I don't think I missed one note! Only the Lord could have made that happen. I got a loud, prolonged standing ovation! (I didn't know that Lisa Perritt was recording me.)[48] And I sold lots of CDs and a few books. Plenty of prayers had been sent up, and all the glory belongs to God.

We made many new friends at the AFA retreat, including Claude and Charlotte Perdue from Kansas. They surprised us by showing up unannounced at our church in Luverne the following Sunday morning (going out of their way). They were sitting by Curtis when I walked into the sanctuary on my way to the piano. My jaw dropped! After the church dinner, they followed us to Petrey to take pictures of us in front of our house. Claude was really impressed with my music. He is a drummer. My promoter husband had me play "Fantaisie Impromptu" for them again. They took some of my CDs and one of my books with them on their journey

---

48 "Revolutionary Etude," played at The Cove, recorded by Lisa Perritt - https://www.facebook.com/lisa.p.perritt/videos/10206669422548232/

home to Kansas. My son-in-law Conrad later recorded me playing this Chopin number on my favorite piano, my Kawai grand, on October 7, 2017. He put it on Facebook, and it received over 3,000 likes and 30 shares! - https://youtu.be/YdZwIXozDDA

After the AFA Retreat I got a call from Randall Murphree, the editor of the AFA Journal. He was at The Cove and heard me play and said he was going to feature me in the first article of the AFA Journal. The December issue arrived at my house on November 29th. I was elated when I read it. Here is an excerpt of the article: ".... Attendees were blessed not only by great speakers and worship leader, Brian Eads, but also by the riveting keyboard artistry of at-tendee, Nancy Petrey.... By impromptu invitation, Petrey took the stage, sat down at the grand piano ... The concert grand piano then exploded with her dynamic rendition of Chopin's 'Revolutionary Etude.' Petrey's piano CD concert **'His Eye is on the Sparrow,'** includes the title song plus *'It is Well With My Soul,' 'Battle Hymn of*

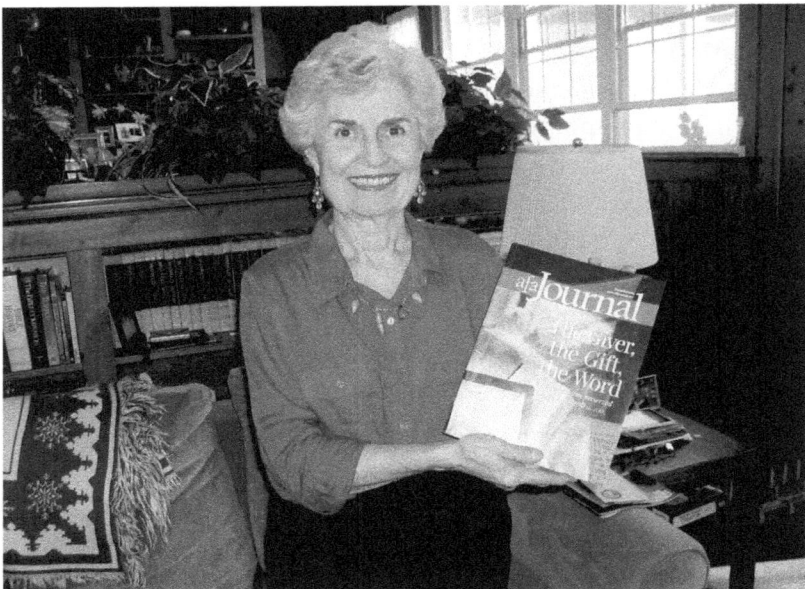

AFA Journal, December 2015 issue, with article on Nancy's piano performance at The Cove

the Republic,' 'As the Deer,' a few classical pieces, and other favorite hymns and worship songs." The article ended with information about ordering the CD. I got a good many orders and appreciated Randall so much for his article.

My fourth time to attend The Cove was in October 2016, and the experience was bittersweet because Curtis had gone to be with Jesus just a few months before. It was the evening of April 7th that Curtis had a heart attack while preparing for bed. He was gone in an instant. I thanked the Lord he did not have to suffer. I had been married to my sweetheart for over 56 years. He had been the "wind beneath my wings." How could I continue without him? I wouldn't call him back, however, because he had grown so weak over the last year. In January 2011, he had been diagnosed with congestive heart failure, but God used our prayers and healed him. In August, Dr. Pat Walker in Luverne examined Curtis and said, "Well, you got your miracle!" Unfortunately, he had another heart attack in January 2012. This time the cardiologists said his death was imminent. Still, he lived on, and God added four more years to his life. But now my best friend, partner in ministry, and beloved husband had come to the end of his race.

Only days before his sudden death I had seen our relative and neighbor, Kline Jeffcoat, out on the walking trail. I was impressed to ask for his cell phone number, in case something might happen to Curtis. He assured me he always answered his phone, even in the middle of the night. He warned that if something did indeed happen to Curtis, that I should call 911 first and then call him and Patsy. So that night when Curtis fell out of the bed, lifeless, I did exactly what Kline said, and help came immediately. Oh, what an awesome God we serve, who goes before us and prepares the way for whatever is coming into our lives.

God's timing is always perfect. Looking back, I can see how God was preparing for Curtis' "graduation," giving him a "last hur-rah," so to speak. Our son Perry and Mickey Brown from Southaven planned a final Homecoming event for Faith United Methodist Church (renamed Life Spring Church) on February 15, 2015. The

Curtis preaching at Faith UMC Homecoming in Southaven, MS, February 2015

building was about to be sold, but this was still holy ground, the place where Curtis was pastor for nine years, and where we experienced the move of God in an awesome way. At the Homecoming, Curtis would preach, and I would lead the singing, just like old times! Susan and Conrad had moved from Texas to Southaven for her to teach at her alma mater, Southaven High, and they had joined Faith. They helped with the event. Perry and Mickey did the cooking.

Jim and Bert attended. Our old members returned, and we had a love feast, so good for the soul! I loved leading the same worship songs we did back in the 1980s (with Susan assisting), and it felt like we had never left. The Holy Spirit was alive and well in our

midst in just the same way. Curtis preached his usual stellar sermon, anointed by the Spirit. Oh, what an unforgettable experience.

A few weeks before Curtis' death, one day out of the blue Dr.

Nancy leading worship at Faith Homecoming

Morgan Moore from Andalusia, Alabama, contacted me about giving a mini-concert at his church, First Baptist, on June 21, 2016. He also wanted me to speak about our Jewish roots at a luncheon following the concert. I was

Curtis & Nancy Petrey and children - Jim, Susan Carriker, Bert, and Perry - at Faith Homecoming

excited to be a "musical Mizpah" again. (Morgan lived across the street from us when David and I were children, and I remember his building us several treehouses.) He had reconnected with Curtis and me, and he and Wilma attended Curtis' funeral. I assured him that I would still speak and give the concert at his church, even though I had not had much time to practice.

My friend whom I went to Israel with in 2012, June White, drove up from Crestview, Florida, to hear me, and that was a blessing. The 9-foot Estonia grand piano was impressive. The concert was 20 minutes long for a group of 35 seniors. I played eight numbers, all but one **by memory,** and ended with "Battle Hymn," the most recently memorized. Jan White made a video of me on the last number.[49] I got a terrific response from both the concert and the message on Jewish roots. After my talk I sold lots of books and CDs. Here I was, a new widow, but my light was still shining brightly as a "messenger girl" for my Lord and Savior, Yeshua the Messiah.

After Curtis was gone, I determined that I still needed to attend the AFA retreat at The Cove that year in October. He would

49  http://bit.ly/BattleHymnNancy

want me to attend. Tricia Richardson, secretary to Don Wildmon at AFA and my dear friend since our days at Faith UMC, agreed

Going to The Cove on AFA van - Nancy, Tricia Richardson, Sue Jarvis, Don & Lynda Wildmon (founders), Tamra & Larry Durham

to be my roommate. We went to Asheville together with others on the AFA van. I was prepared to play the piano if I was called upon. This time, if asked, I would play "Battle Hymn of the Republic," arranged by Marilynn Ham. I had played it twice by memory already, at the concert in Andalusia and at my church on September 11, 2016. Tim Wildmon did call me up to the stage, and I performed the "Battle Hymn." My sweet friend Tricia closed her eyes and interceded for me the entire time I played. The audience gave me a standing ovation. Glory to God and heartfelt thanks to Tricia.

I played again in the chapel, "Jesus Loves Me" (based on "Clair de Lune"), arranged by Fred Bock. After the 2015 AFA Retreat at The Cove, Curtis had "commanded" me to memorize this beautiful piece, so I obeyed and was able to play it several times by memory after that. God showed me I could do it, so I memorized "Battle Hymn" also.

Practicing for performance at The Cove, October 2016

Performance of "Battle Hymn of the Republic" at The Cove

I wish Curtis had been in Andalusia and at The Cove to see me play. He loved musical performances and especially enjoyed watching the Gaithers perform on T.V. He delighted in seeing his wife, children, and grandchildren perform, too, but he turned out to be quite a musical performer himself! Beginning at Faith UMC in Southaven, Curtis had occasionally promised from the pulpit that if certain conditions were met by the members, he would sing a solo! He always laughed when he said it because he was anything but a singer, or so he thought. I had to remind him that the Lord gave him a beautiful voice once he surrendered to preach in 1976. Well, he finally made good on his decades-old promise back in September 2013, at our church for the morning worship service. Only our Minister of Music, Buddy Johnson, and Brother Mike Green knew it was going to happen. I had asked the children to pray for Dad but didn't tell them why. Curtis felt like God wanted him to do this, so he summoned the courage and took a leap of faith. He kept saying he might back out, but I encouraged him that God would hold him up, to just trust in Him. He sang a medley interspersed with testimony, and he did it a cappella – "Fill My Cup," "He Touched Me," "Something Beautiful," and "My Tribute." The congregation joined us as I played the final chorus. People complimented him and said they were touched and blessed. At almost 74 years of age, my wonderful husband "walked on water." I could not have been prouder.

Curtis recognized talent when he saw it, and Susan has talent. She has a rich, alto voice. When she visited us, he would insist she sing at our church. One of his favorites was *"Follow Me"* by Kelly Willard, and she always "knocked it out of the park!" Curtis really enjoyed arranging concerts. I kidded him about being my agent, but he was also a promoter for our whole family. He had blessed our community in Luverne and beyond by arranging a concert by Song Yang and family (see Chapter 30). Now he would arrange a Petrey Family Concert at South Luverne Baptist Church. All of our family would be coming for Thanksgiving 2015, and most of them would be there on the Wednesday night before, which was open on the church calendar. We didn't expect a large audience because of the date, but there were about 50 of us. Curtis was the master of ceremonies.

Curtis, master of ceremonies for the Petrey Family Concert at South Luverne Baptist Church, November 2015

I played Curtis' favorites, "Fantaisie Impromptu" and "I Rise Up to Worship" ("Chariots of Fire" melody), which Susan helped me sing. I also played "No One Ever Cared for Me Like Jesus," arranged by Marilynn Ham. Our son Perry played his guitar and sang his favorite, "Beautiful to Me" by Don Francisco. (My favorite song Perry sings is "Steeple Song" by Don Francisco.) Conrad played guitar, and our daughter Susan and he sang "The Lord is My Shepherd," "I Believe in Jesus," and "The Revelation Song." Perry's children, P.J. and Zoe, with P.J. playing guitar, sang "Oh How I Need You" and "Great are You, Lord." Perry's son Joshua on the piano and wife Kara sang "Can't Help Falling in Love with You" and "The Book of Love." Our son Jim, accompanied by our son Bert and Conrad on guitars, sang "More of Jesus." Bert played guitar and sang "Have You Seen Jesus?" written by our cousin Bob McLeod.

The congregation joined us for the final number, singing "How Great Thou Art." Curtis was bursting with pride to present his family in concert, and the audience loved the music. Both of us were so proud that several of our grandchildren – P.J. and Kelly, Anna Duhe, and Joshua & Kara – are worship leaders in their churches. Joshua is a professional teacher and worship leader at Gateway Church in Dallas. All these children are gifted musically and love the Lord.

Perry has eight children, including his and Liv's little boys, David and Benjamin. Perry's oldest son Franco and his wife Kara C. have four children, and Perry's daughter Anna and her hus-

Petrey family (left side of stage) singing "How Great Thou Art"

band Nate have a toddler, another Benjamin. That makes five great-grandchildren for me! No doubt these youngest ones will also join our throng in making music to the Lord. I am one blessed mother, grandmother, and great-grandmother!

Petrey family (right side of stage)

The day after the concert on Curtis & Nancy's porch in Petrey - Nate & Anna Duhe, Isaiah, Zoe, Jim, Perry, Conrad & Susan Carriker, Joshua & Kara, Kelly & P.J.

My promoter husband was a matchmaker. He had inspired the marriage of our grandson P.J. and Kelly Geoghagan, and he officiated at their wedding. He also encouraged our son Jim to go ahead, follow his heart, and marry Robyn Stewart. I

Jim & Robyn's family of ten with Robyn's parents, Eric & Vonnie Stewart, and Nancy - July 16, 2016. (left side): Adin and Joshua Marmon, Madeline Petrey, Callison Marmon; (right side): Taylor, Trey, and Hannah Petrey, Justus Marmon

wasn't so sure for three reasons – Robyn lived in Texas, Jim lived in Georgia, and they **each** had four children! Curtis was planning to officiate at their wedding in Petrey on July 16, 2016, but God had other plans. The wedding went on, and I played the piano and prayed a blessing over Jim and Robyn (in Hebrew and English, the Aaronic benediction, Num. 6:24-26). Surely, Curtis was rejoicing from the ramparts of heaven, as Rev. Cliff Cobb joined Jim and Robyn in marriage.

Robyn's children are also musically talented. Adin plays French horn, and Callison has been a dancer and now sings in the school honor choir; so does Madeline. Robyn's four children increase my number of grandchildren to 17 now! Our entire "musically-loaded" family came to Petrey to visit after Christmas 2016, and we numbered 33!

Entire Petrey family in Petrey, Alabama, December 27, 2016 - 33 people

My promoter husband, who inspired ten people to enter full-time ministry during our days at Faith UMC, had continued through life to promote his family, especially me. On his 74th birthday, December 16, 2013, I wrote an abbreviated biography of his life, since he became my husband. Here is the final paragraph:

*I am really thankful for the way Curtis has changed my life. If I had married someone else, I may have missed the excitement of going to several foreign countries, doing mission work, leading church praise teams and choirs, and even knowing how to operate a computer! I wouldn't have lived in so many different towns and made so many fantastic friends. I wouldn't have these wonderful children and grandchildren and be able to live in such a peaceful little town as Petrey. Curtis encourages my music ministry, especially playing the piano, always "promoting" me and insisting I play for family and friends when they visit. Praise God for Curtis Petrey and that he is my husband!*

Nancy promised "Whither thou goest I will go" (Ruth 1:16), and she did for 56 years of marriage!

My life would never have shined so brightly for Jesus without Curtis. I look forward to receiving the same "promotion" he received that night he graduated to heaven, and we can be reunited in ETERNAL LIGHT! In the meantime, I am "aged wine," letting my light shine! The Light of the World lives inside me. To **Him** belongs all the glory. **HE** is the Light that shines!

# APPENDICES

# My Song Compositions

I have included scores for a few of my song compositions in this book for anyone who is interested in playing and/or singing them. Most of my songs, only words, not music, are already in my book, *Habitation of Honey: Poems and Songs* (Gonzalez, Florida: Energion Publications ©2015). There are also four songs with the scored music in another book, *The Honeycomb is Waiting: Poetic Devotionals* (Gonzalez, Florida: Energion Publications ©2016).

In this book I have musical scores for seven of my songs. One, *"A Merry Heart,"* I scored for this book. The others I had already notated by hand on staff paper but had never published.

1. *"Take Time to Smell the Roses,"* May 1981, revised July 27, 1989
2. *"A Merry Heart,"* April 27, 1989

**Three** songs from *Heaven's All Astir (A Christmas musical)* performed by children at Golden Triangle Trinity Church, Columbus, Mississippi, in 1994 – A play about the birth of Christ viewed from the angels' perspective in heaven. Denise Collins: script writer, director, and choreographer. Nancy Petrey: **six** original songs, music and words.

3. *"Jericho Stomp!"* October 28, 1994
4. *"Heaven's Ablaze,"* October 28, 1994; verses 2 & 3 – January 31, 2015
5. *"The Savior's Looking Up at Me,"* October 26, 1994

6. *"Messenger,"* June 4, 1995
7. *"The Wedding Feast (You are Aged Wine),"* June 12, 1995 ©October 23, 1995: revised September 13, 2009

## Take Time to Smell the Roses

Child:

1. Take time to smell the ros-es, Mom —. Take time to hold my hand —. Take time to hear my
2. Take time to smell the ros-es, Dad —. Take time to talk with me —. Take time to let me

prob-lems —and — to say you un-der-stand —. Take time to play a game —with— me, to
hug your neck, take time to real-ly —see — that I am grow-ing up — so —fast, I

throw and catch a ball —. Take time to say you love — me —, and to see I'm — grow-ing
need your help each day — to guide me in the things I do — at- school and — church and

CHORUS

— tail —. Take time to smell the ros-es — when they're bloom-ing —. Take time
— play —.

to smell the ros-es — when they're there —. Take time to smell the ros —es—

when they're bloom-ing—; For I'm your rose —, please show me that— you — care. —

3. Mom:
   I'll take the time to hold your hand.
   I'll take the time to hear.
   I'll take the time to understand.
   My child, you are so dear.
   I'll take the time to play with you.
   My love for you is true.
   Please take the time to pray for me,
   obey, and love me, too.

4. Dad:
   I'll take the time to talk with you.
   I'll take the time to love.
   I'll notice that you're growing fast.
   I'll seek His help above
   To guide you in the things you do
   At school and church and play.
   Please pray for me that I will live
   for Jesus ev'ry day.

CHORUS (Parents)

I'll learn to smell the roses when they're blooming.
I'll learn to smell the roses when they're there.
I'll learn to smell the roses when they're blooming;
For you're my rose, I'll show you that I care.

July 27, 1989

Words and music by Nancy Petrey ©2018

## A Merry Heart

A merry heart doeth good like a medicine,
A merry heart doeth good for my soul. I open wide
my mouth, and He fills it; I open wide my heart, He re-vives it
I sing a song that I have never heard be-fore ——. A merry heart
doeth good like a medicine, A merry heart doeth good
for my soul. He satisfies my mouth with good things
so that my youth is renewed like the eagle's, and I am lifted up on the
wings of a brand new song! He brought me up — out of a horrible pit
and out of the miry clay. He set my feet up—on a rock
and established me in His way ——. For He hath put a new song in my mouth,
even praise unto our God — Many shall see it and

(Based on Proverbs 17:22; Psalms 81:10; 103:5; 40:2-3; 103:4)

April 27, 1989                                    **Words and music by Nancy Petrey ©2018**

## Jericho Stomp!

From "Heaven's All A'Stir," a Christmas musical for children

(Little angels dance with a boogie beat.)

CHORUS

The Jer-i-cho Stomp! You could hear it for miles a-round! The Jer-i-cho Stomp! Mi-chael went out on — the town! The Jer-i-cho Stomp! It made a might —y sound —! The Jer-i-cho Stomp! It made the walls fall down!

VERSE

Josh-u-a said, "The bat-tle plans — have come from the Heaven-ly Chief!" He said, "You just walk it, Don't you dare talk it. Take my Ark a-round the town, on-ly the trum-pets will sound. A day at the time, six days in all—, sev-en times on the sev-enth day—." The ang-els all poised, wait-in' for the noise. Came the shout! And they be-gan to sway—!

October 28, 1994                    Words and music by Nancy Petrey ©2018

## Heaven's Ablaze

From "Heaven's All A'Stir," a Christmas musical for children

(Little angels waltzing vigorously and singing)

Heav-en's a-blaze with His glo-ri-ous birth! Heav-en's a-glow with a wonder-ful mirth! An-gels are twirl-ing and ca-vort-ing in space! Shin-ing in the bright-ness of the smile on God's face! Hal-le-lu-jah! Hal-le-lu-jah! Hal-le-lu — jah! Hal-le-lu-jah! Hal-le-lu-jah! Hal-le-lu — jah! Hal-le-lu-jah! Hal-le-lu-jah! Hal-le-lu — jah! Hal-le-lu-jah! I'm prais-in' the Lord!

2. Jesus, our Savior, came into this world –
   Glory from heaven in Mary unfurled!
   He made His entrance in God's plan of grace,
   Shining in the brightness of the smile on God's face!
   (Chorus)

3. Joseph had dreamed of an angel in bed –
   "Name the wee baby 'Yeshua'", he said.
   "He'll save His people, their sins He'll erase,"
   Shining in the brightness of the smile on God's face!
   (Chorus)

October 28, 1994 (verses 2 & 3, 2016)

Words and music by Nancy Petrey ©2018

## The Savior's Looking Up at Me

From "Heaven's All A'Stir," a Christmas musical for children

(Little angel looks down from the portals of heaven at baby Jesus in the manger.)

The Savior's look-ing up at me, I ask my-self, how can it be that God Al-might-y sent His Son to earth a ba-by boy? As I look down in-to His face, I see His glo-ry and His grace. How can this Low-ly One be bring-ing so much joy to me? The an-gels ap-plaud His marv-e-lous ma-jes-ty. The fin-gers so ti-ny once formed you and me. The feet that once stood be-side the throne of God are ly-ing in a man-ger in a cat-tle stall! The Sav-ior's look-ing up at me, I ask my-self, how can it be that God Al-might-y sent His Son to earth a ba-by boy? As I look down in-to His face, I see His glo-ry and His grace. How can this Low-ly One be bring-ing so much joy to me?

October 26, 1994                      Words and music by Nancy Petrey ©2018

## Messenger

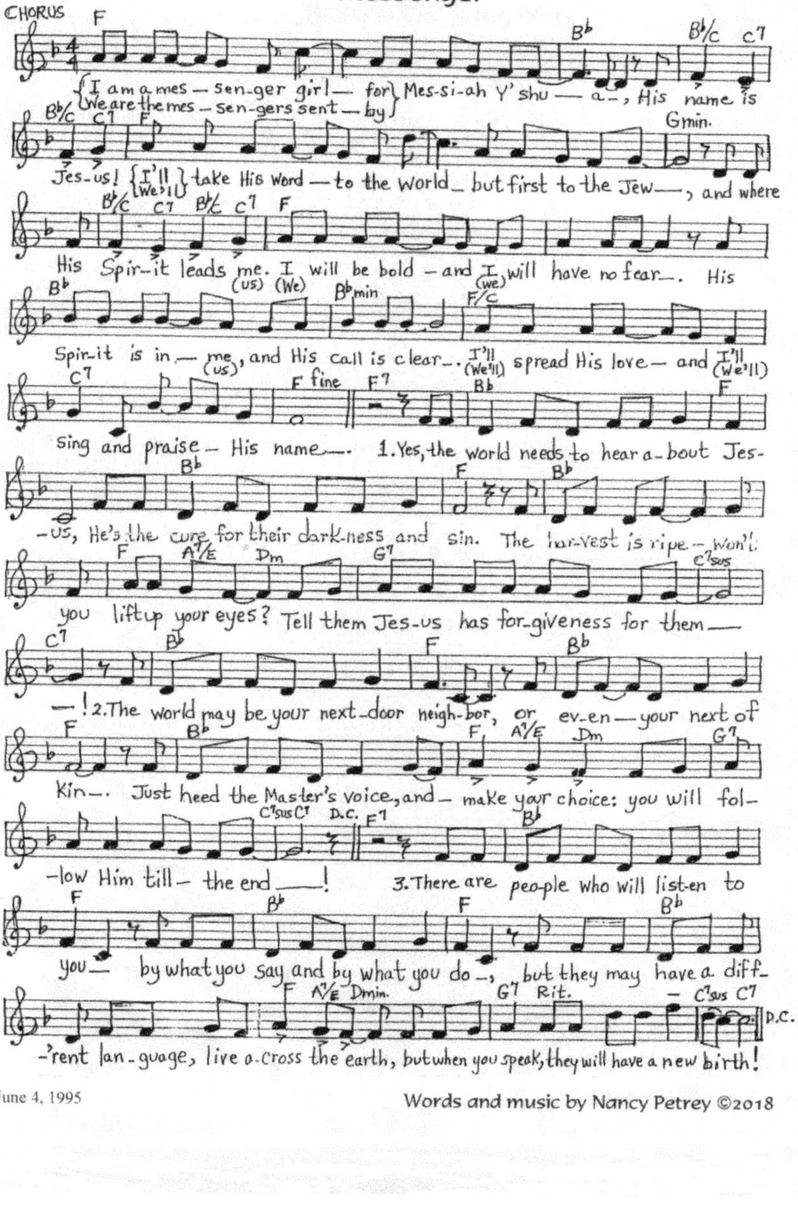


June 4, 1995

Words and music by Nancy Petrey ©2018

## The Wedding Feast
### (You are Aged Wine)

1. Have you ev-er heard the sto-ry of the wed-ding—in Ca-na— of Ga-li-lee—? Have you thought much a-bout the stone pots that were used for the wine—? They were sit-ting there wait-ing to be used; they had great ca-pac-i-ty—. But till Je-sus came they were emp-ty as they could be—. There was a wed-ding—, and Jesus had them filled to-the brim— with wa—ter—. He said "Draw some out. Take it to the mas-ter of the feast—." When the mas-ter of the feast tast-ed—the wa-ter that was made in-to wine—, he called the Bride-groom and said, "What you have done is — so ver-y fine—." 2. The world serves their best wine at the first and saves—the worst till last—, but Je-sus has a bet-ter i-dea—: He ag-es— His wine—. And as the days grow long, and you don't feel so strong, He will come to you——, fill you up with Liv-ing wa-ter, and He'll change you in-to fin-est wine—.

CHORUS ten. F G⁷ / F/c C Am 3 ten.
You are aged wine... I've been sa-ving you a long—— time—. You are aged

F G⁷ / C 3 ten. F G⁷
wine. You are a won-der and a sign—. You are aged wine—. To ev'ry thing there is

F/c C Am / Dm G⁷
a sea-son and a time—. The Bride-groom has had a long-fast! He's saved

C-F-C C⁷ F / Dm
the ve-ry best till last—! 3. You were that wa-ter pot that was emp-ty till

G⁷ C / Am Dm
Je-sus came your way——. At the wed-ding of your spi-rit, you were

G⁷ C C⁷ F
filled with Liv-ing Wa-ter, what a hap-py day——! Now He'll pour you out—,

Dm G⁷ C Am Dm
and you'll quench the thirst of a dy-ing world—— He's saved the best

G⁷ C-F-C C 3 ten. F G⁷
till last—. You're the finest wine that He has—! You are aged wine—.

F/c C Am 3 ten. F G⁷
I've been sav-ing you un-til the end of time—. You are aged wine—. You are a

C 3 ten. F G⁷ F/c
won-der and a sign——. You are aged wine—. The King is coming soon, He'll say, "You are

Am Dm G⁷ C-F-C
Mine—. The Bridegroom at last will have His bride, and He'll call you to His side—. He'll take you

Dm G⁷ C-F-C Dm
up in-to the air—. for this day you must pre-pare. On His throne in new Jerusalem——

G⁷ - - - -
for the wedding Feast of the Lamb——!

June 12, 1995 – Revised September 13, 2009

Words and music by Nancy Petrey ©1995

# The Purposes of Music

Music is one of the most powerful forces in the world. It is a universal language. It is eternal and was with God at the Creation. When He laid the foundations of the earth, *"the morning stars **sang** together."* (Job 38:7) Among all the gifts God has given His earthly creatures, music must be the highest and best. It grieves me that so often it is prostituted for fame, financial gain, and indulgence in fleshly passions, with no regard for the Author's feelings. The highest use of music is in worshiping God. Once I tried to make a recording of "harmless" secular songs, combined with a few sacred songs that I loved to sing, and it turned out to be a failure. My trusted critics (knowledgeable family members) said that all but four songs were off-key! My little pet project had bombed. I didn't want to admit it, but, evidently, the Author of music wasn't too excited about mixing His songs with the world's songs. I am not saying that it is wrong to sing and play secular music, but in my case, God wouldn't let me combine them with His songs. Before you begin to think I never enjoy anything but gospel or "church" music, please see Chapter 23.

In my childhood and teenage years, I discovered that music is good therapy. The McMaster Institute for Music and the Mind has found that "Music impacts our mind and our body in ways that we are only just beginning to understand. It really does 'soothe the savage breast,' lowering blood pressure, reducing anxiety, helping us feel connected, even easing pain."[50] That is true, but even if scientists can measure it and analyze it, it can't be experienced apart from God. It is His gift to us, and He doesn't show partiality. Jesus said, *"…He makes His sun rise on the evil and on the good, and sends rain on the just and on the unjust."* (Matthew 5:45) God lavishly bestows the gift of music on all His creatures. Music touches the

---

50  https://www.research.mcmaster.ca/research-matters/music-soothes-the-savage-breast

deep recesses of our hearts and brings His love, joy, and peace. In gratitude let us go to the Bible and see how we can please this awesome Giver of good gifts.

Music, instruments, songs, and singing are mentioned innumerable times in the Scripture. To get an idea of God's purposes for music take note of these examples:

(1) After the Israelites crossed the Red Sea, Moses taught them a victory song to sing to the Lord. Miriam, his sister, led the women with timbrels and dancing. (Exodus 15)

(2) Deborah, a judge and prophetess of Israel, led in battle with Barak against their enemies and defeated them. After their victory, Deborah and Barak sang a song, rehearsing the victorious battle. (Judges 5)

(3) David, the shepherd boy, played his harp, and sang to God as he tended the sheep. He played his harp in the palace, and evil spirits departed from King Saul. Later, as King of Israel he made musical instruments for use in the tabernacle in Jerusalem for the priests to praise and worship God around the clock. He brought the Ark of the Covenant to Jerusalem with trumpets, tambourines, and sounding cymbals. (1 Samuel 16:23; 2 Chronicles 7:6; 1 Chronicles 15:25-29) King David wrote most of the Psalms, and they are filled with exhortations to sing and praise God. *"Come before His presence with singing."* (Psalm 100:2)

(4) King Solomon wrote 1005 songs (1 Kings 4:32). His book, Song of Solomon, is introduced as "the song of songs which is Solomon's" (1:1). Many Bible scholars say the romance between Solomon and the Shulamite maiden is a picture of the love of Christ for His bride, the church. The great number of songs Solomon composed indicate the importance God gives to music.

(5) When the prophet Elisha was about to prophesy, he called for a musician. The musician played, and the hand of the Lord came upon Elisha. He was enabled to prophesy the battle strategy for Israel against Moab. Israel carried out God's directions through the prophet and defeated Moab! What a fascinating story. (2 Kings 3:15-27)

(6) Probably the most well-known story in the Bible about the power of music in battle is that of King Jehoshaphat sending out the choir in front of the army. The singers praised God at the top of their lungs, and the enemy armies turned on each other. Israel's army only needed to mop up at the end, dividing the spoil. After they blessed the Lord, the king led all the people back to Jerusalem *"with stringed instruments and harps and trumpets, to the house of the Lord."* (2 Chronicles 20:1-30)

(7) On the night Jesus was arrested, He and His disciples had partaken of the Passover meal. "Then He took the cup, and gave thanks, and gave it to them, saying, 'Drink from it, all of you. This is my blood of the new covenant, which is shed for many for the remission of sins ... and **when they had sung a hymn, they went out to the Mount of Olives.**" (Matthew 26: 27-30) That night in the Garden of Gethsemane Jesus prayed so fervently that he sweated great drops of blood. No doubt the singing of a hymn had helped to prepare Him for what was ahead.

(8) In the New Testament we are exhorted to "be filled with the Spirit, speaking to one another in psalms and hymns and spiritual songs, singing and making melody in your heart to the Lord" (Eph. 5:19). "Let the word of Christ dwell in you richly in all wisdom, teaching and admonishing one another in psalms and hymns and spiritual songs, singing with grace in your hearts to the Lord." (Colossians 3:16)

(9) Paul and Silas were imprisoned in Philippi for casting a demon out of a fortune teller, which caused her masters to lose their livelihood. Paul and Silas were beaten, and their feet were put in the stocks. They began to pray and sing hymns, praising the Lord at midnight. God sent an earthquake, set them free, and the prison doors opened! (Read full story in Acts 16:16-38)

(10) The Ark of the Covenant was brought into Solomon's newly-built temple. When the trumpet players and singers praised and thanked the Lord *"as one,"* the temple was filled with a cloud! It was the glory of God! The priests couldn't even continue ministering because of the cloud! (2 Chronicles 5:13)

From these examples we can see God's purposes for music. He obviously wants us to celebrate our victories with music. He wants us to take pleasure in His gift of music. We can get direction from Him **for** our battles and praise Him **in** the battles. Music is an avenue through which we can be filled and re-filled with the Holy Spirit. We can drive out evil spirits when we sing or play under the inspiration of the Holy Spirit. We can be strengthened and prepared for trials that are coming upon us. We can be set free from literal and spiritual imprisonment. Music can help plant the Word of God in us. Best of all, we can let God's love flow through us and back toward Him, as well as toward others, when we sing and play instruments. However, the highest use of music is to worship the Author of music. When we praise Him with one accord, His glory covers us! Let my light shine for You, dear Lord, always!

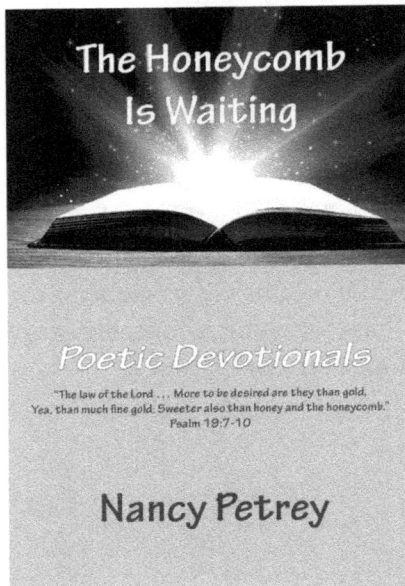

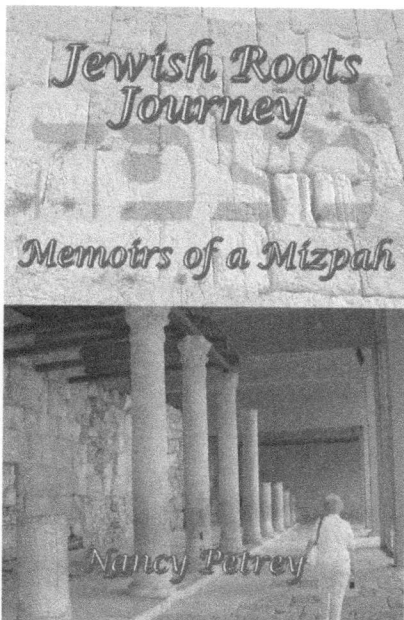

As you follow Nancy on her journey you will be entertained, challenged, and inspired.

**NANCY PETREY**

Many modern Christians have forgotten that Jesus, the authors of the Bible, and the first church were all Jewish. Therefore, they do not understand the New Testament correctly.

WHY CHRISTIANS SHOULD CARE
ABOUT THEIR
**JEWISH ROOTS**

Topical
Line
Drives

Volume 17

$\Sigma$